C000185412

The
Travelling I

John Wesley in the
North-East of England
1742-1790

With details also of the work
of Charles Wesley and other
early Methodist preachers

First Edition 1987

© Revised Edition 2003, The Wesley Historical Society, North-East Branch

Published by The Wesley Historical Society, North-East Branch and printed by Methodist Publishing House

ISBN 1 85852 236 6

FOREWORD TO THIS NEW EDITION

To the North East England Branch of the Wesley Historical Society there could be no finer way to mark this year's worldwide celebration of the 300th anniversary of the birth of John Wesley than to reissue Geoffrey Milburn's classic study of Wesley's travels through our region. When it was first published in 1987 copies were quickly sold. Now in this celebration year we would like to make it available to a wide range of new readers. We are delighted that our partnership with the Methodist Publishing House has enabled this to be achieved.

The tension between central direction and local decision making is very much a contemporary issue for government, public services, and business and community. So too in the eighteenth century with John Wesley and the development of Methodism. In those days before the advent of the railways, the car, the telephone, mass media and the internet, John Wesley's regional tours had a crucial role to play in the underlining of central authority whilst recognising developing local responsibilities.

Then as now the North East maintained a distinctive regional identity even in times of dramatic economic and social change. We are proud of our direct links with the Travelling Preacher, not least through our heritage of a number of chapels dating from the time of his visits. We hope that Geoffrey Milburn's historical study will not just satisfy our fascination with the past but will inspire us to be active participants in the living history of the Church's ongoing response to the changing needs of the Age.

John Wearmouth
New Year's Day 2003

John Wesley
painted by the Sunderland artist Thomas Horsley, 1784

FOREWORD TO THE ORIGINAL EDITION

Those who listened to the series of talks given by Geoffrey Milburn on Radio Newcastle in 1985 will give a warm welcome to their appearance in print; and an equally warm welcome will be given by those who did not hear them. I heard some of the talks, but regretfully missed others, so I now not only welcome their publications, but cordially commend them to others, especially to those who find the history of Methodism in the North-East such a fascinating story. It was a delight to have that story presented to us through the medium of Geoffrey's pleasing voice (we can hear it, yet miss it, as we read) but the written word now preserves in print all the excitement and frustration, the heroism, the grace and the glory of the 'first fine careless rapture' of those heady days.

It is all there – Wesley at Sandgate, The Orphan House 'without (outside) a city wall', Grace Murray and John Bennet with Brother Charles the wrecker (what a story!), Hindley Hill, Keenley, Jacob Rowell and his pocket books, Sunderland, the Dales . . . well, read it and see! Quotations are well chosen, often in Wesley's own words, and always nicely illuminating the incidents or scenes under consideration.

Thanks to Geoffrey for writing and thanks to the Branch for publishing this excellent book. We covet for it a wide sale, both in the North-East and beyond.

Revd Dr. John C. Bowmer
1911-2000
W.H.S. N.E. President 1977-2000

PREFACE TO THE ORIGINAL EDITION

The year 1988 will see the 200th anniversary of the death of the evangelist and hymn writer Charles Wesley (19th March) as well as the 250th anniversaries (21st and 24th May respectively) of the conversions both of Charles and of his brother John Wesley, the "travelling preacher" from whom this book takes its title. These anniversaries will be commemorated (not only by Methodists) throughout Britain and also in many places overseas, since Methodism, which in large part is the fruit of these two men's work, is now a worldwide Church. It is hoped that this little book will serve to explain, at least with reference to the north-east of England, why the 1988 anniversaries carry so much interest and significance.

The chapters of the book consist of 10 out of an original 12 talks which were broadcast by BBC Radio Newcastle during 1985. The intention of the series was to allow John Wesley in particular, but also his brother Charles and other early Methodists, to speak for themselves by the use of the extracts from their own journals. Apart from minor alterations the talks are printed as they were transmitted, retaining the character of the spoken word. In the broadcasts the extracts were read by Peter Hudson, with Virtue Jones adding the women's voices; it is hoped that in this printed form they will convey the same vivid sense of the reality of the past as Peter and Virtue were able to impart in reading them.

For those who would like to know more, references are given at the ends of the chapters (see page x for the abbreviations used); there is also a pretty comprehensive guide to further reading at the end of the book.

Thanks are due to many people who have made the book possible; to Harry and Margaret Batty for an invitation to spend a holiday in 1984 at their home (at that time the Methodist manse in Reeth) where much of the preparatory reading was done; to Virtue Jones who encouraged me in writing the talks and produced them for Radio Newcastle; to my wife Mary, and to Barbara Peebles, for invaluable help with typing; to Tom Cawley for many useful tips on the printing of the book and Martin Vagoni of NBS Services for his professional advice; to the Editor of the Epworth Press, 1 Central

Buildings, Westminster, for permission to quote from the Standard Edition of John Wesley's Journal; to the North East branch of the Wesley History Society for agreeing to publish the book;   to Northern Arts for generous assistance towards the cost of printing; and finally to the Revd Dr John Bowmer for his Foreword as well as for kindness and encouragement in other ways.

Geoffrey E. Milburn
February, 1987

ILLUSTRATIONS

Cover picture:
The illustrations on the cover of this book and on the title page are copies of a drawing by Tom Sterling of the bronze equestrian statue of John Wesley, by Gordon Walker R.A., which stands outside Wesley's Chapel (The New Room) in the Horsefair, Bristol. The statue's many authentic features are clearly visible, including the open book in Wesley's hand, the loose rein with which he generally rode, and (as Dr. Luke Wiseman noted on unveiling the statue in 1933) the 'intelligent look on the face of the horse'! Mr Edmund S. Lamplough donated the statue. It was he also who purchased the New Room in 1929, and presented it back into the ownership of the Wesleyan Methodist Conference out of whose hands it had passed over a century earlier.

CONTENTS

ABBREVIATED REFERENCES

Journal: The Journal of the Rev. John Wesley AM,
                        edited by Nehemiah Curnock in 8 vols., 1909-
                        1916, reprinted 1938.

Life of C.W.:   The Life of the Rev. Charles Wesley, M.A., by
                        Thomas Jackson, 2 vols., 1841.

E.M.P.:   The Lives of the Early Methodist Preachers,
                        edited by Thomas Jackson in 3 vols., 1837-
                        1838 published in 6 vols. 1865, and similarly in
                        1871.

Wesley's Veterans: Wesley's Veterans: Lives of the Early
                        Methodist Preachers told by themselves, with
                        additions and annotations by John Telford, in
                        7 vols., c.1910-1914.

                        (The two works immediately above contain
                        substantially the same material but in a
                        different sequence.)

Hampson: Memoirs of the late Rev. John Wesley, A.M.,
                        with a Review of His Life and Writings, by
                        John Hampson, 3 vols., 1791.

Steele: History of Methodism in Barnard Castle and
                        the Principal Places in the Dales Circuit, by
                        Anthony Steele 1867.

Stamp: The Orphan House of Wesley with Notices of
                        Early Methodism in Newcastle upon Tyne and
                        its Vicinity, by William W. Stamp, 1863.

I

THE TRAVELLING PREACHER

JOHN WESLEY'S ARRIVAL
IN NEWCASTLE 1742

On an evening towards the end of May in the year 1742 two clergymen rode on horseback across the ancient medieval bridge spanning the River Tyne and entered Newcastle for the first time. Their names were John Taylor and John Wesley, and though the first of these is now virtually forgotten it was in part through his agency that his famous companion John Wesley came to be in the north-east at all. Taylor was a preacher employed by a remarkable aristocratic lady, the Countess of Huntingdon, who used her wealth and influence to promote Christian work and evangelical preaching in eighteenth century England. She naturally took a great interest in Wesley, and knowing the leading role he had been playing in the religious revival in London and the south-west she urged him to extend his preaching to other areas and in particular to visit and preach to 'the colliers of the north'.[1] Wesley had to spend a few days with the Countess in Leicestershire in May 1742, and at the end of that stay he set off northwards, with John Taylor as his companion, to fulfil her request, a request which was certainly in harmony with his own keen desire to seek any new opportunities to take the message of the Christian faith to the people of England and especially to the working classes and the poor.

Having arrived in Newcastle the two sought lodgings at a hostelry which stood in relatively open country outside the Pilgrim Street gate, on the north side of the old town where busy Northumberland Street is today. By a strange coincidence this inn must have stood very near to where the first Methodist chapel, the so-called Orphan House, was later to be built. Having taken refreshment, the two Johns walked down into the town to look around. John Wesley was not impressed:[2]

I was surprised: so much drunkenness, cursing and swearing (even from the mouths of little children) do I never

1

remember to have seen and heard before in so small a compass of time. Surely this place is ripe for Him who 'came not to call the righteous, but sinners to repentance'.

Wesley came to see that there was a different side to Newcastle life and character in due course! On Saturday they probably continued their inspection of the town, but on Sunday Wesley's work began in earnest. Let us hear his account of it, taken from his journal:

Sunday 30 May: At seven in the morning I walked down to Sandgate, the poorest and most contemptible part of the town, and standing at the end of the street with John Taylor, began to sing the hundredth psalm. Three or four people came out to see what was the matter, who soon increased to four or five hundred. I suppose there might be twelve to fifteen hundred before I had done preaching; to whom I applied those solemn words: 'He was wounded for our transgressions, he was bruised for our iniquities: the chastisement of our peace was upon Him; and by His stripes we are healed'.

Observing the people, when I had done, to stand gaping and staring upon me with the most profound astonishment, I told them: 'If you desire to know who I am, my name is John Wesley. At five in the evening, with God's help, I design to preach here again'.

The sermon which those astounded Geordies heard early on that Sunday morning might be described as the first Methodist sermon preached in the north-east of England. If you walk along the modern quayside in Newcastle, where the open-air market is held on Sundays, you will find at the far end, near the old Milk Market, an obelisk which was erected in the later nineteenth century to record this occasion, and to mark the spot, or near to it, where Wesley stood as he preached. A little way above the obelisk, on the steeply sloping hillside, is the Keelmen's Hospital. And at five o'clock Wesley stood near the Hospital and preached again as promised:

At five the hill on which I designed to preach was covered from the top to the bottom. I never saw so large a number of people together, either at Moorfields or at Kennington Common. I knew it was not possible for the one half to hear, although my voice was then strong and clear; and I stood so as to have them all in view, as they were ranged on the side of the hill. The word of God which I set before them was 'I will heal their backsliding, I will love them freely'. After preaching, the poor people were ready to tread me under foot, out of pure love and kindness. It was some time before I could possibly get out of the press. I then went back another way than I came; but several were got to our inn before me, by whom I was vehemently importuned to stay with them, at least a few days; or however, one day more. But I could not consent, having given my word to be at Birstall, with God's leave, on Tuesday night.

Wesley could not complain of the size of his congregations – some 1,500, in the morning and more in the evening, crowds big enough to call to his mind the great gatherings at the popular open-air preaching places in London, Moorfields and Kennington Common. How did Wesley command these enormous numbers on his first visit to Newcastle? Partly because the spot he chose was close to the most densely populated part of the town at that time, with a network of narrow lanes and courts running northward from the riverside. There were certainly plenty of people in the crowded tenements to provide a potential congregation. It's true that very few of them were likely to see the inside of a church on a Sunday, but a parson preaching out of doors was another matter. In fact to the ordinary folk of Newcastle it must have seemed incredible! What was the man up to? So they came out of curiosity and amazement, and gaped and stared as Wesley relates. But something else happened. The message this parson was preaching, and the manner in which he preached it, got through their astonishment and scepticism, and touched their hearts. This is the really remarkable thing that happened that day, and it must in large part be explained by the character and commitment of that remarkable man, John Wesley.

Wesley was 39 at the time. He was the son of a Church of England parson, Samuel Wesley, Rector of Epworth in Lincolnshire; and his brother Charles was a parson also. Though not a wealthy family they had been able to send their sons to public school and Oxford University where John, who was a good scholar, became a Fellow of Lincoln College. Had his life run in different channels he might have devoted himself to study and teaching and writing. Things were to be different but it's important to remember that Wesley never lost his love of learning or his belief that reading good and serious books is important for everyone. He continued to read voraciously himself, but in his busy life as a preacher most of his reading had to be done on horseback. It is interesting to read in his journal that on his journey to Newcastle he was reading Xenophon's Memorable Things of Socrates (in English, probably, though he could have read it equally well in Greek) and when he left the town he was buried in an old theological work in Latin.

Wesley's background and training therefore were clerical and studious. His voice was the voice of the cultured classes. His manner, dress and demeanour were sober, neat and respectable. What was a man like this doing preaching in the Newcastle slums at seven o'clock on a May morning? The short answer is that he, and also his brother Charles, had both experienced deeply moving evangelical conversions within a few days of each other in May 1738. For both men this experience transformed their understanding of their role as priests, and they commenced an open-air itinerant ministry to take the Christian Gospel to the growing numbers of ordinary English folk who for all sorts of reasons had little or no contact with the churches.

This ministry as a travelling preacher lasted for the rest of John Wesley's life. For over 50 years after his conversion he was incessantly on the move, preaching to all who would listen, doing much to revive vital religion in England and elsewhere, and also (but not intentionally) laying the foundations of what was to become the Methodist Church. This was 'Mission England' in an eighteenth century context, conducted not in football stadiums, but in the highways, market squares and village greens of English towns and villages.

Let us try to picture the man himself. We can get help here from someone who knew Wesley well and who wrote the first biography of him, published in Sunderland in 1791, the year Wesley died. The author was John Hampson, at that time Curate in charge of St. John's chapel of ease in the east end of Sunderland, and later to be Rector of Sunderland. Hampson had been one of Wesley's travelling preachers, but left him in 1785 and entered the ministry of the Church. He was a good deal younger than Wesley so knew the great man best in his later years. However, his vivid description of

Wesley shows us all the qualities which those Newcastle folk must have discerned when they heard him for the first time in 1742:[3]

John Wesley, a portrait painted by John Williams about the time of Wesley's first visit to Newcastle

Selina, Countess of Huntingdon

The figure of Mr. Wesley was remarkable. His stature was of the lowest; his habit of body, in every period of his life, the reverse of corpulent and expressive of strict temperance and continual exercise. And notwithstanding his small size, his step was firm, and his appearance, till within a few years of his death, vigorous and muscular. His face, for an old man, was one of the finest we have seen. A clear, smooth forehead, an aquiline nose, an eye the brightest and most piercing that can be conceived, and a freshness of complexion scarcely ever to be found at his years and impressive of the most perfect health, conspired to render him a venerable and interesting figure. Few have seen him without being struck with his appearance; and many, who had been greatly prejudiced against him, have been known to change their opinion the moment they were introduced into his presence.

In his countenance and demeanour there was a cheerfulness mingled with gravity; a sprightliness which was the natural result of an unaccustomed flow of spirits, and yet was accompanied with every mark of the most serene tranquillity. His aspect, particularly in profile, had a strong character of acuteness and penetration.

In dress he was a pattern of neatness and simplicity. A narrow plaited stock, a coat with small upright collar, no buckles at his knees, no silk or velvet in any part of his apparel, and a head as white as snow, give an idea of something primitive and apostolical; while an air of neatness and cleanliness was diffused over his whole person.

His rank as a preacher is pretty generally understood. His attitude in the pulpit was graceful and easy, his action calm and natural, yet pleasing and expressive, his voice not loud, but clear and manly, his style neat, simple and perspicuous, and admirably adapted to the capacity of his hearers.

That is an impressive description as I think you will agree. John Hampson had obviously watched Wesley closely and admiringly, and brings his subject to life before our eyes. His account is particularly convincing since Hampson was not an uncritical admirer of Wesley and in other parts of his biography had less flattering things to say about some aspects of his character, especially his love of authority.[4]

This is the man then who made such a strong impact upon Newcastle on his very first visit, with people so moved that they crowded round him and nearly crushed him 'out of pure love and kindness' as Wesley himself put it. Warm emotion was no doubt important and welcome. But Wesley knew that if his work was to have lasting effect it needed firm foundations, good organisation and discipline. To achieve all that he would have to return at greater leisure, and devote himself in a painstaking way to the work.

Let us, in closing, picture Newcastle at this time.[5] It was in many ways medieval in its physical features, dominated by the great castle with its Norman keep, encircled by the town walls with their fortified gates, served by the four ancient parish churches, and entered from Gateshead across the old bridge, lined with houses and shops, which had stood since the fourteenth century. The population of about 20,000 was still crowded chiefly into the low parts along the river, where Wesley preached, and which he referred to as the poorest and most contemptible part of the town. Some well-to-do merchants in fact still had houses here but most of those who could do so had moved into the more attractive areas, especially Westgate Street and Pilgrim Street. There was also some overspill outside the walls into the early suburbs, especially the suburb of Sandgate inhabited mainly by keelmen.

Newcastle was in many ways a prosperous and proud community, with rich merchants, professional men, scholars and skilled artisans and tradesmen. But it was also a town caught up in economic change and population growth, with a growing army of poor, and inadequate social services. In times of stress and food shortages the social tensions could become acute, law and order break down, and desperate mobs terrify the respectable middle classes. Religious zeal which had burned brightly if also dangerously in the previous century was now largely spent and the established churches and the handful of dissenting meeting houses had little appeal for the majority. It was into this situation that Wesley came in 1742, and that one brief visit in May of that year must have been enough to make him well aware both of the challenges and the opportunities facing him in Newcastle. In fact he was destined to return there something like 50 times during the next half century, and the story of this work, together with that done by Charles Wesley and other preachers, will form the basis of the remainder of this book.

REFERENCES

1. *Journal, iii, 9 n.*

2. *Ibid., 13.*

3. *Hampson iii, 166-69.* It is interesting also to read the following on pp.178-79: *His manner in private life was the reverse of cynical or forbidding. It was sprightly and pleasant to the last degree, and presented a beautiful contrast to the austere deportment of many of his preachers and people, who seem to have ranked laughter among the mortal sins. It was impossible to be long in his company without partaking his hilarity . . . His cheerfulness continued to the last, and was as conspicuous at fourscore as at one and twenty.*

4. *See for instance Hampson iii, 202 ff.*

5. *See S. Middlebrook, A History of Newcastle-upon-Tyne (1968), Chapter XII.*

II

INTRODUCING CHARLES WESLEY
AND CHRISTOPHER HOPPER

Having left Newcastle on 31st May 1742 after his first brief visit, John Wesley was not free to return until November of that year. We may well imagine that before leaving he would give advice to earnest enquirers as to how they might apply his teaching and make their Christianity real and practical. But many remained simply mystified by his visit and did not know what to make of it all. We have this on the authority of a contemporary, Christopher Hopper, a young native of Ryton on Tyne who was employed on the local colliery wagonways, and who later became one of the best of Wesley's assistant preachers. It is interesting to learn from his short autobiography that news of Wesley's first visit spread very rapidly up the Tyne valley to the area in which Hopper worked:[1]

> *In May 1742 we heard a strange report of one Wesley, a Church clergyman, that had been at Newcastle upon Tyne, and had preached in Sandgate to many thousands, who heard him with astonishment. This new thing made a huge noise. The populace entertained various conjectures about him; but few if any could tell the motive on which he came, or the end he had in view. He made a short blaze, soon disappeared, and left us in a great consternation.*

The next stage in the work was in fact undertaken not by John Wesley but by his brother Charles who paid an extended visit to the north-east in the early autumn of 1742, leaving a few days before John's arrival on 13th November. Charles Wesley was a few years younger than John, and though he was independent and outspoken and no respecter of persons, he always regarded his elder brother as in some special way the divinely appointed leader of the Methodist revival and respected him for that high calling. In the early years of the revival Charles was as active as John in travelling and preaching but fairly soon settled down to a more stable and stationary ministry, in Bristol then in London. Nevertheless he paid seven visits to the north-east between 1742 and 1751, did much courageous pioneering work, and was the first of the two brothers to spend any length of time in the region.

In chapter one we heard a description of John Wesley by the ex-Methodist Curate of Sunderland, John Hampson. Let us hear now how Hampson described Charles:[2]

> *This gentleman was of a warm and lively disposition, of great frankness and integrity; and there was an honesty in his nature which some would perhaps call precipitancy and imprudence, and which would not suffer him to pass over, or to bear with, anything his judgement disapproved. He had a great regard for men of principle in all persuasions; and with his whole heart abhorred a hypocrite, and the whole tribe of sycophants and flatterers; nor could persons of such character be long in his presence with impunity. His conversation was pleasing and instructive and often seasoned with wit and humour. His religion was of the right sort, not gloomy and cynical but cheerful and benevolent.*

It is surprising that this somewhat 'John Bullish' man also had strong musical and poetic inclinations. The music came out mainly in his two sons who were very talented musicians and composers, and in his grandson, the well known Victorian composer of church music, Samuel Sebastian Wesley. It is as a religious poet and hymn writer that Charles Wesley himself is still best remembered today, and the numbers of those who have sung and loved his great hymns – 'Jesus, lover of my soul', 'O for a thousand tongues to sing', 'Thou God of truth and love', 'Let earth and heaven combine', 'Hark, the herald angels sing', 'O thou who camest from above' and so on – must be incalculable. Many of his hymns were composed on horseback, being jotted down in rough, or memorised, and written down when the journey was over. There are stories of Charles dismounting and rushing into the house calling for pen, paper and ink to write out a hymn before it slipped from his memory. In his journal for May 1743 we find this entry:[3]

> *Near Ripley my horse threw and fell upon me. My companion thought I had broken my neck, but my leg only was bruised, my hand sprained and my head stunned – which spoiled my making hymns, or thinking at all, till the next day when the Lord brought me safe to Newcastle.*

That was Charles' second visit. Let's go back to his first in the autumn of 1742. This was of great importance but there is no account of it by himself. However, we know the main outlines of it.[4] Being a visit of several weeks duration Charles was able not only to preach but to establish a number of Societies for seekers and converts. The Societies met regularly for fellowship, prayer, mutual support and direction, and of course for worship in which hymn singing and preaching were central. They therefore gave order and continuity to the evangelistic work done by the Wesleys. Without these Societies there would have been little permanence. They were also the source from which lay helpers were recruited. The Wesleys were insistent that a Society was not a Church, nor a rival to the Church of England. They hoped that Christians in the Societies would also preserve links with their mother Churches and attend church, especially for the Sacrament. Eventually, however, the Societies developed such a strong sense of their own identity that a separation from the Church became more and more inevitable; but that is looking ahead.

In that autumn of 1742 Charles Wesley preached much in Newcastle, in Sandgate, in Newgate prison, and in the inner courtyard (or Square) of the recently built Keelmen's Hospital which formed a very convenient and sheltered open-air preaching place. A Society was formed in Newcastle which soon had 250 members and continued to grow. Among its members were keelmen, shopkeepers, sailors, artisans of various trades, poor working folk, and a sprinkling from the respectable middle class and lesser gentry.

It was Charles Wesley also who first fulfilled the Countess of Huntingdon's urgent request to visit 'the colliers of the north'. From his base in Newcastle he made preaching forays out to Swalwell, Tanfield, Whickham and Ryton and here also Societies were formed. We have an eyewitness of this work, Christopher Hopper:[5]

Charles Wesley,
younger brother of John Wesley

Christopher Hopper

Charles (Wesley) came, and preached at Tanfield Cross; I ran with the multitude to hear this strange preacher. When I saw a man in a clergyman's habit, preaching at a public cross to a large auditory, some gaping, some laughing, and some weeping, I wondered what this could mean. When he had concluded some said, 'He is a good man, and is sent to reform our land'; others said, 'Nay, he is come to pervert and deceive us, and we ought to stone him out of our coasts.' I said, 'If he is a good man, good will be done, and it is plain we want a reformation; but if he is an imposter, he can only leave us as he found us, that is, without hope and without God in the world.' I cannot tell what induced me to go so far; but I found I was in danger of being called a Methodist, and was glad to dismiss the conversation with a smile and piece of drollery.

We will stay with Christopher Hopper for a little while because he serves very well as a model or type of many other early Methodists. The name Methodist was in fact first used to describe a religious society at Oxford University led by John and Charles Wesley. It was later used as a term of derision for those who joined the Societies which grew up as a result of the Wesleys' travelling preaching. The implication of the word was that Methodists lived by method, that is

11

they had rules and discipline and took their religious obligations seriously. This kind of earnestness was not popular, and certainly was usually misunderstood. Hopper was aware that to be known as a Methodist would lead to difficulties, so although he felt drawn to the movement he tried to resist its attraction. But eventually his resistance was overcome, and he was converted. The results were dramatic:[6]

> *I then found a glorious and undeniable change. God, Christ, angels, men, heaven, earth, and the whole creation appeared to me in a new light, and stood related to me in a manner I never knew before. I found love to my God, to His yoke, to His cross, to His saints, and to His friends and enemies. I said, 'This is Bible religion, scriptural Christianity; let men call it what they please – "a delusion," "enthusiasm," "Methodism," or "Mahometanism" – that is nothing to me; hard names do not change the nature of the thing.' I then went on my way rejoicing – a wonder to my father's family, to all that knew me, and to myself. All my idols fell to the ground before the ark of God. I found a perfect hatred to sin, and a complete victory over it.*

> *The whole tenor of my life and conversation was new. Free grace, infinite mercy, boundless love made the changes. My heart, my tongue, my hands, were now, in my little way, employed for my loving God. I was no longer of the world; therefore the world began immediately to hate me. Some said, 'Ah! what think you? Christopher Hopper is converted.' Others said, 'He hath received the Holy Ghost.' Others said, ' He is mad, keep far from him; come not near his habitation.' Some, of a more compassionate turn, pitied me; but all agreed I had renounced my baptism, left the Church, and was in a dangerous situation.*

Hopper was very soon recruited as a leader for the new Society formed by John Wesley at Low Spen and was led on naturally into the ranks of the lay preachers, later becoming a full-time travelling preacher. We will meet him again in our story.

Charles Wesley left Newcastle early in November 1742 and a few days later John arrived to develop the work in the town and the region round about. It is not surprising that the Wesleys were so anxious to cultivate Newcastle. In their nationwide strategy they knew the importance of good bases. London was the obvious centre for the south and east, and Bristol for the south-west and midlands. For the north the advantages of Newcastle were obvious. An important town in itself, it was also a focal point of important routes and a centre from which preaching forays could readily be made to other northern towns, to many colliery communities, to the Pennine dales busy at that time with lead mining, and northwards into Northumberland and Scotland.

The high regard the Wesleys had for Newcastle is reflected in the amount of time they devoted to it, especially in the crucial early years of the Revival. From his second visit in November and December 1742 to 1746 John Wesley spent something like 260 days in and near the town – that is about one-fifth of his time. This was the most concentrated attention he ever devoted to Newcastle, though he still continued to visit it frequently during the rest of his life. And in addition to those 260 days spent by John Wesley in Newcastle between 1742 and 1746, Charles spent another 180, never overlapping with his brother. In other words, one or other of the Wesley brothers was in and around the town for just about one third of those four years. During that time Methodism in Newcastle, and indeed in the north-east as a whole, was put on firm foundations.

The physical and mental demands on the Wesley brothers of these constant journeyings and preachings, not to mention the anxiety of caring for the newly formed societies, was, of course, very great. One formidable difficulty in the winter months was the north-east weather. In December 1742 John Wesley sat in his lodgings in Newcastle and wrote:[7]

> I never felt so intense cold before. In a room where a constant fire was kept, though my desk was fixed within a yard of the chimney, I could not write for a quarter of an hour together without my hands being quite benumbed.

If sitting in a freezing room was bad enough, travelling through wild and wintry conditions was desperately difficult. The winter of 1744-1745 was particularly severe and both brothers suffered from it. Let us hear first from Charles:[8]

> November 18th: I walked to Sunderland from Newcastle, and back again. The storm of hail and snow was so violent

that I was often going to lay me down in the road, unable either to walk or to stand.

November 22nd: I rode from Newcastle to Spen being so feeble that I could not walk, yet I was forced to it in the last mile, being almost starved to death in the next to impassable ways. I was led, I know not how, by the brethren, up to the knees in snow, the horses often sinking up to their shoulders . . . I was surprised at the great number got together in such a season.

The following February John Wesley had to battle through heavy snowstorms as he travelled up the old Great North Road from Sandhutton in Yorkshire to Newcastle. The experience moved him to some dramatic descriptive writing:[9]

Saturday 23rd: We found the roads abundantly worse than they had been the day before, not only because the snows were deeper, which made the causeways in many places impassable (and turnpike roads were not known in these parts of England till some years after) but likewise because the hard frost, succeeding the thaw, had made all the ground like glass. We were often obliged to walk, it being impossible to ride, and our horses several times fell down while we were leading them . . . It was past eight before we got to Gateshead Fell, which appeared a great pathless waste of white. The snow filling up and covering all the roads, we were at a loss how to proceed, when an honest man of Newcastle overtook and guided us safely in to the town. Many a rough journey have I had before, but one like this I never had, between wind and hail and rain and ice, and snow and driving sleet and piercing cold. But it is past.

REFERENCES

1. *E.M.P.* i, 195.

2. Hampson i, 56-57.

3. *Life of C.W.* i, 332-33. It is interesting to read Thomas Jackson's comment on Charles Wesley's character, in connection with his decision to retire in 1757 from itinerant preaching and from active

involvement in the oversight of the Methodist movement: 'He appears to have thought it the best course for him to retire and leave the people and preachers in the hands of John, whose talents for government were of the highest order. Charles could write hymns with a facility and a power which no man of his age could equal; and few could surpass him as an awakening and effective preacher; but he had no aptitude for controlling and harmonising the discordant spirits of men. For the maintenance of discipline in cases of difficulty his faculties and habits were not at all suited. His uprightness, generosity and the kindness of his heart were unquestionable but his impetuosity created prejudice, and left a soreness in the minds which his brother could easily conciliate and direct' Life of C.W., ii, 136.

4. See for instance Stamp, pp.4-10.

5. E.M.P. i, 185-86.

6. Ibid. 189-90.

7. Journal iii, 55.

8. Life of C.W. i, 406-7.

9. Journal iii, 165.

III

THE NEWCASTLE ORPHAN HOUSE

From 1744 John Wesley used to call together his full-time helpers to meet in an annual conference at which the affairs of Methodism were frankly discussed. Wesley himself directed the proceedings and minutes were later published in the form of questions and answers, which sound very much like the voice of Wesley himself, though no doubt they express the mind of the brethren as well. Here is one example:[1]

> Q. What may we reasonably believe to be God's design in raising up the preachers called Methodists?
>
> A. Not to form any new Sect; but to reform the Nation, particularly the Church; and to spread scriptural holiness over the land.

This is a particularly interesting minute. In Wesley's eyes the Methodist Societies, such as those which were being established in Newcastle and the communities round about, were ancillaries to the Church of England, and certainly did not constitute a new independent sect. Wesley was never in his own eyes a dissenter, and he always professed loyalty to the Church of England of which he was a priest. His brother Charles was even more adamant on this point than he was. When in Newcastle the Wesley brothers worshipped regularly at one of the parish churches, usually St. Andrew's or All Saints, and encouraged the Methodists to do so too. Yet it must be admitted that Wesley's innovations apparently ran counter to the Church of England or, at least, challenged its usual practices. In Wesley's eyes rules, even Church rules, were made to be broken when the work of God demanded it. So the alliance of his vigorous new movement with the old established Church was an uneasy one and in many places it broke down altogether. If the Church had possessed more breadth of sympathy and had been ready to support Wesley's mission then perhaps Methodism might have become a renewal movement within it. As it was, the two drifted apart though the rift was not formalised until after Wesley's death.

The reasons for this are complex but one very powerful factor was the highly organised vigour and close fellowship of the Methodist Societies, which came to be regarded by most members as their all-sufficient spiritual home, so that the ministrations of the Church of England were less valued. This was strongly reinforced when the Societies acquired their own meeting places. These 'preaching houses' (the word chapel was not used at first) soon became the focal points of Methodist activities and loyalties, and they pulled the Methodists more and more away from the Church despite Wesley's intentions to the contrary.

The first Methodist preaching house in the north-east was begun under Wesley's direction in December 1742, on a site outside the Pilgrim Street gate in Newcastle, on what is Northumberland Street today. A plaque on the front of a shop tells the passer-by that the old building stood there, though no trace of it now remains. Brunswick chapel, a little lower down Northumberland Street, is the direct heir of the old preaching house, which was known as The Orphan House since it had originally been Wesley's intention to use it partly to accommodate orphaned children. This plan never materialised, but the building was, as we should say, a multi-purpose one, and a description of it offers an interesting insight into the character of early Methodism. Here is how the Revd William Stamp described it in his book on the Orphan House published in 1863:[2]

The Orphan House Newcastle, built 1742-43.

17

The lower part of the 'House' was the chapel, fitted up with pulpit and forms; the men and women sitting apart. Galleries were subsequently erected; the entrance to which, in 1790, was by a broad staircase on the outside, commencing at the left corner of the space in front, and leading to a covered way above. Above the chapel was a large compartment lighted from behind, the centre of which was used as a band-room; opening from which, on either side, were several class-rooms for the use of the Society. On the highest storey – a kind of Scotch 'flat' – were suites of apartments, subsequently appropriated for the residence of the preachers and their families; while on the roof was a wooden erection, about eleven feet square, with tiled covering, generally known as 'Mr. Wesley's study'. A narrow staircase, little more than two feet wide, led from the preachers' dwelling below, to a small floor in the actual roof of the building, opening from which was the doorway to the study. This apartment, even in the tidiest days of the Orphan-House, must have been of the most homely description. The fire-place would, in this day, be repudiated by the most humble cottager. In strict keeping with it were the door and furniture of the room. Its exposure to the wintry blasts of the north would also render it an undesirable retreat for any to whom warmth and comfort were matters of moment. Such, however, was the apartment designed and appropriated by the self-denying Wesley for his special residence when sojourning in Newcastle. Here, at different periods, much of his valuable time was spent: here also, as various intimations in his Journal show, he loved to be.

This quaint rambling old building was in fact only the second purpose-built Methodist chapel to be erected, the first having been built a year or two before in Bristol. Those who visit Bristol are strongly urged to go to see Wesley's Chapel there, in the old Horse Fair. It is still referred to by its original Wesleyan name of the New Room. This is what these early chapels were – rooms to preach in, and places where the Society could meet in Bands and Classes for fellowship. And at the New Room there still can be seen, over the chapel proper, the domestic quarters used by Wesley and his fellow travelling preachers. There are few places which evoke more powerfully the spirit of those pioneering days of early Methodism, and it takes only a little imagination to see the preachers coming in, muddy and tired from their travels, and excitedly sharing their experiences of the work of God at a welcome meal round the plain wooden table. We can only regret that the Orphan House no longer exists to stir such memories in a north-eastern setting.

Those who joined the Methodist Society in Newcastle, or anywhere else, had a strict code of conduct to live up to, since Wesley was firm in believing that committed Christians should live disciplined lives and renounce worldly behaviour. This in itself demanded a good deal of dedication and effort, and on top of that criticism and ridicule from outsiders had also to be endured. In the fact of all this not all members were able to maintain their commitment, and either left the Society of their own accord, or were expelled for breaking the Rules. In March 1743 Wesley went through the membership lists of the Newcastle Society and made some very revealing comments:[3]

> *I observed the number of those who had left the society since December 30 was seventy-six:*
>
>> *Fourteen of these (chiefly Dissenters) said they left it because otherwise their ministers would not give them sacrament.*
>>
>> *Nine more because their husbands or wives were not willing they should stay in it.*
>>
>> *Twelve, because their parents were not willing.*
>>
>> *Five, because their master and mistress would not let them come.*
>>
>> *Seven, because their acquaintance persuaded them to leave it.*
>>
>> *Five, because people said such bad things of the society.*
>>
>> *Nine, because they would not be laughed at.*
>>
>> *Three, because they would not lose the poor's allowance.*
>>
>> *Three more, because they could not spare the time to come.*
>>
>> *Two, because it was too far off.*
>>
>> *One, because she was afraid of falling into fits.*
>>
>> *One, because people were so rude in the street.*

THE

NATURE, DESIGN, AND GENERAL RULES

OF THE

UNITED SOCIETIES,

IN LONDON, BRISTOL, KINGSWOOD, NEWCASTLE-
UPON-TYNE, &c.

———

1. In the latter end of the year 1739, eight or ten persons came
to me in London, who appeared to be deeply convinced of sin,
and earnestly groaning for redemption. They desired (as did two
or three more the next day) that I would spend some time with
them in prayer, and advise them how to flee from the wrath to
come ; which they saw continually hanging over their heads.
That we might have more time for this great work, I appointed
a day when they might all come together, which from thencefor-
ward they did every week, namely, on Thursday, in the evening. To these, and as many more as desired to join with them,
(for their number increased daily,) I gave those advices, from
time to time, which I judged most needful for them ; and we
always concluded our meeting with prayer suited to their several
necessities.

2. This was the rise of the United Society, first in London,
and then in other places. Such a society is no other than " a
company of men having the form and seeking the power of god-
liness, united in order to pray together, to receive the word of
exhortation, and to watch over one another in love, that they
may help each other to work out their salvation."

3. That it may the more easily be discerned, whether they
are indeed working out their own salvation, each society is
divided into smaller companies, called *classes*, according to their
respective places of abode There are about twelve persons in

*The first page of Wesley's Rules for his Societies,
first published in Newcastle, 1743*

Two, because Thomas Naisbit was in the society.

One, because he would not turn his back on his baptism.

One, because we were mere Church of England men. And,

One, because it was time enough to serve God yet.

The number of those who were expelled from the society was sixty-four:

Two for cursing and swearing.

Two for habitual Sabbath-breaking.

Seventeen for drunkenness.

Two for retailing spirituous liquors.

Three for quarrelling and brawling.

One for beating his wife.

Three for habitual, wilful lying.

Four for railing and evil-speaking.

One for idleness and laziness. And,

Nine and twenty for lightness and carelessness.

This is a very interesting catalogue. Those who left the Society of their own volition offer very human and understandable reasons – opposition within their own families, adverse public opinion, ridicule, inconvenience, lack of time and so on. What Thomas Naisbit had done to cause offence to two of the members is not known! There are also hints of undue pressure, or even a kind of blackmail, employed by the dissenting ministers who excluded those who attended Methodist meetings from the sacrament of Holy Communion, and by parish officials who threatened loss of the weekly poor allowance for the same reason. The reasons for expulsion also reveal very human failings, some admittedly serious but many apparently slight, especially the expulsion of twenty-nine members for 'lightness and carelessness'.

Being a Methodist was a serious business! But the rules and the discipline were only one side of Methodism. The chief emphasis was on conversion, on a change of heart and lifestyle, on a new sense of joy and freedom, and a strong desire for holy living. This more inward side to Methodism was, of course, stressed in the preaching services at the Orphan House, as well as in the prayer meetings and the meetings of the classes and the bands into which the Society was divided. In the highly charged atmosphere of these gatherings, when Wesley was urging salvation and holiness on his flock, the psychological pressures could become so powerful that some of the worshippers started to groan, to shout out, to shake and even to drop to the ground in an apparent faint. John Wesley did not set out deliberately to provoke this excited and enthusiastic response but he was prepared to take it very seriously, and not dismiss it or even discourage it.

He conducted an enquiry among those who had been affected in this way and discovered the following:[4]

1. *That all of them were persons in perfect health and had not been subject to fits of any kind till they were thus affected.*
2. *That this had come upon every one of them in a moment while they were hearing the word of God or thinking on what they had heard.*
3. *That in the moment they dropped down, they lost all their strength and were seized with violent pain.*

Having heard all this Wesley came to his own conclusions:

These symptoms I can no more impute to any natural causes than to the Spirit of God. I can make no doubt but it was Satan tearing them as they were coming to Christ. And hence proceeded those grievous cries whereby he might design both to discredit the work of God and to affright fearful people from hearing the word whereby their souls might be saved.

Charles Wesley took a less credulous and distinctly more sceptical view than his brother about what he described as 'the fits'. He arrived in Newcastle on 30th May 1743, about two months after John had left, and found that the enthusiasm and bodily excitement were still persisting. Immediately he set about discouraging these phenomena:[5]

4 June: Some stumbling blocks, with the help of God, I have removed, particularly the fits. Many no doubt were at our first preaching struck down, both body and soul, into the depth of distress. Their outward affections were easy to be imitated. Many counterfeits I have already detected . . . One girl, as she began to cry, I ordered to be carried out. Her convulsions were so violent as to take away the use of her limbs, till they laid her and left her without the door. Then immediately she found her legs and walked off. Some very unstill sisters, who always took care to stand near me and try which could cry the loudest, since I had them removed out of my sight have been as quiet as lambs.

One very practical advantage of these measures was noted by Charles 11 days later:[6]

I observed at Newcastle that many more of the gentry come now that the stumbling block of the fits is taken out of their way.

That's an interesting comment. Obviously some of the respectable and well-to-do folk of Newcastle were being attracted to Methodism at that very early date, despite the fact that the movement's main evangelical thrust was at first to the poorer classes. This perhaps is not surprising. John and Charles were, after all, men of the educated and cultured middle class, and priests of the Church of England. The interest of the well-to-do in Methodism, and even, in some cases, their active support of it, was obviously very helpful to the Wesleys. In due course the respectable middle class became very influential in Wesleyan Methodism. It was they, for instance, who built the splendid big chapels such as Sans Street in Sunderland in 1793 and Brunswick in Newcastle in 1820. They never constituted the majority of the movement but they certainly helped to give it social acceptance and status. They also created some problems. Was Methodism to be a popular lively movement, free and spontaneous, appealing to the workers? Or was it to be more controlled and orderly, acceptable to the middle class? Or could it be both? We see this dilemma nicely illustrated in Charles' anxiety to eradicate the 'fits' which had offended the gentry. The problem went on raising its head in other ways later on. It affected Methodism in the towns most of all. In the countryside things could be different – and especially in the pit villages, and it was Methodism among the miners that we shall consider in the next chapter.

REFERENCES

1. *Minutes* 1811, p.3.

2. *Stamp, pp.16-18* (an earlier and more detailed description of the Orphan House can be found in *Proceedings of the Wesley Historical Society* vol. xx part 6, June 1936). In 1857 the old Orphan House was demolished and replaced by a new building devoted to Sunday School work. A final service was held in the old building on 10th September 1856. The congregation gathered in the lower part of the old chapel but the other parts were thrown open to public inspection including the galleries (disused for 30 years), the band room, the domestic apartments, and Mr. Wesley's study. On this occasion someone recalled how after the mid-week preaching service at the Orphan House the Society members repaired to the Band Room upstairs and sang a hymn there together, before dividing into the several smaller classrooms, thus 'avoiding the sadly discordant effect produced by the concurrent singing of several classes in close proximity to each other.' (Stamp, pp. 244-45).

   When the Orphan House was taken down in 1857 the material of Wesley's study (a wooden structure about 11 feet square with a tiled roof) was carefully preserved and afterwards sold, for the benefit of the School Bazaar Fund, to Mr. Solomon Mease of Cleveland House, North Shields, in whose grounds it was re-erected in its original form. (Stamp, p.16n.)

   During her evangelistic tour of the north in 1859-60, Mrs. Phoebe Palmer, an American preacher, stayed with the Mease family at North Shields. On 17th December 1859 she sat in Wesley's study (in the Meases' garden) and wrote a letter to friends in America describing the revival and how Mease himself had 'received a blessed baptism of the Spirit at one of our afternoon services'. Her mind obviously returned to the scenes associated with the building in which she was sitting: 'Here is the veritable place where Wesley penned many of the precious things which have been blessed to thousands in Europe and America, and will continue to be prized yet more and more till the end of time.' Richard Wheatley, *The Life and Letters of Mrs. Phoebe Palmer,* 1881/1984, p.359. Mrs. Palmer's daughter, Phoebe Palmer Knapp, composed tunes for religious songs, including 'Blessed Assurance', (668 in *Hymns & Psalms).*

3. *Journal, iii,* 70-71.

4. *Ibid.,* 69.

5. *Life of C.W. i,* 33-34.

6. *Ibid.,* 335.

IV

AROUND THE PIT VILLAGES

Everyone in the north-east knows of Peterlee, the new town in County Durham which has grown up since World War II. Those, however, who know the town may not always know that it is named after a famous Durham miners' leader who was also a Methodist lay preacher. Peter Lee and his friend Jack Lawson (later Lord Lawson) are two particularly well known, and fairly recent, examples of men who combined a deep commitment to trade unionism and politics with a sincere and active attachment to Methodism.[1] Very many other instances could be quoted, going back into the early years of the nineteenth century. The commitment of many north-eastern miners to Methodism goes back even further than that, to the days of John Wesley himself. Let us look at how it began.

Wesley's very first venture into open-air evangelism had, in fact, been among the coal miners of Kingswood, near Bristol, in 1739. Working among them taught him some important lessons. The first was about himself – he learned that he had a peculiar talent for popular preaching, and could magnetise an audience, even one of rough uneducated folk standing out of doors in all weathers. Secondly, he came to see that people like this, living in their separate communities, often despised, and usually neglected by the churches, were not impervious to the Christian message if it was presented to them clearly and forcefully by someone they could trust and respect. Moreover, Wesley realised that the miners were no different from, nor less intelligent than, the rest of the population, but usually lacked the encouragement and amenities for education and self-improvement.

Wesley never forgot his Kingswood experiences and the lessons learned there. And he was eager to apply them in the north-east, as soon as the opportunity presented itself, which was not, in fact, until his third visit, in the early months of 1743. The first actual mention of miners in his north-east journal is on 1st March of that year:[2]

I preached at two at Pelton, five miles south of Newcastle.
A multitude of people were gathered together from all the

neighbouring towns, and (which I rejoiced at much more) from all the neighbouring pits. In riding home I observed a little village called Chowden, which they told me consisted of colliers only. I resolved to preach there as soon as possible.

He was back at Pelton about a fortnight later:

As I was preaching in Pelton, one of the old colliers, not much accustomed to things of this kind, in the middle of the sermon began shouting amain, for mere satisfaction and joy of heart. But their usual token of approbation (which somewhat surprised me at first) was clapping me on the back.

That conjures up a lively picture! Other pit villages began to be included in his schedule; two such were Birtley and South Biddick on the Wear, where Wesley describes an open-air preaching:

Tuesday 22nd March: I went to South Biddick, a village of colliers seven miles south east of Newcastle. The spot where I stood was just at the bottom of a semi-circular hill, on the rising sides of which many hundreds stood; but far more on the plain beneath. I cried to them in the words of the prophet 'O ye dry bones, hear the word of the Lord!' Deep attention sat on every face; so that here also I believed it would be well to preach weekly.

Wesley had already made that same resolve with regard to the place he calls Chowden, known to us better as Chowdene. This is now part of suburban Gateshead, high on the fell side on the south of the town, but in Wesley's day it was a pit village in open country, on the edge of the old Gateshead parish. His first visit was on 8th March:[3]

In the afternoon I preached on a smooth part of the Fell (or Common) near Chowden. I found we were got into the very Kingswood of the North. Twenty or thirty wild children ran round us, as soon as we came, staring as in amaze. They could not properly be said to be either clothed or naked. One of the largest (a girl about fifteen) had a piece of ragged, dirty blanket hung about her, and a kind of cap on her head of the same cloth and colour. My heart was exceedingly enlarged towards them; and they looked as if they would have swallowed me up, especially while I was applying those words 'Be it known unto you, men and brethren, that through this man is preached unto you forgiveness of sins'.

'The very Kingswood of the North' says Wesley of Chowdene – that is to say, an out and out mining community such as that he had known in the Bristol area. Modern history tends to think that the older view of the pit villages of the 18th and 19th centuries as places of isolation and degradation was exaggerated, the result of respectable middle-class reactions and misunderstandings. Nevertheless, it would be hard to deny that life in some of them was raw and rough. Wesley gives this impression at Chowdene and also at Plessey in Northumberland which he first visited on Good Friday 1743. Plessey was in the Blyth valley to the south of Bedlington, and, as at Chowdene, there is no trace today of the busy mining community which once was here. When Wesley says that the miners here were renowned for 'savage ignorance and wickedness of every kind' we may feel that he himself is in part expressing the prejudices of polite society, and exaggerating the sins of the miners in order to highlight the transformation brought about by the evangelical revival. Nevertheless, if this is really how he viewed Plessey it was courageous of him to preach there in the first place with so little hesitation.

The Wesleyan Chapel at Low Fell, Gateshead, built in 1754.
The building no longer stands.

Let us hear his own account:[4]

> *April 1st (being Good Friday) – I had a great desire to visit a little village called Plessey, about ten measured miles north of Newcastle. It is inhabited by colliers only, and such as had been always in the first rank for savage ignorance and wickedness of every kind. Their grand assembly used to be on the Lord's day, on which men, women and children met together to dance, fight, curse and swear, and play at chuck ball, span farthing, or whatever came next to hand. I felt great compassion for these poor creatures, from the time I heard of them first; and the more because all men seemed to despair of them. Between seven and eight I set out with John Healy, my guide. The north wind, being unusually high, drove the sleet in our face, which froze as it fell, and cased us over presently. When we came to Plessey, we could very hardly stand. As soon as we were a little recovered I went into the Square and declared 'Him who was wounded for our transgressions' and 'bruised for our iniquities'. The poor sinners were quickly gathered together and gave earnest heed to the things which were spoken. And so they did in the afternoon again, in spite of the wind and snow, when I besought them to receive Him for their king, to 'repent and believe the Gospel'.*

> *On Easter Monday and Tuesday I preached there again, the congregation continually increasing. And as most of these had never in their lives pretended to any religion of any kind, they were the more ready to cry to God as mere sinners for free redemption which is in Jesus.*

It is one of the mysteries of the eighteenth century revival that men and women of the working classes who were pretty well divorced from all organised religion responded to evangelical preaching in the way Wesley describes here. In part this must be attributed to the qualities of Wesley and the other preachers; in part also to the dangerous lives of many at that time and the constant proximity of death, a factor which was powerful in mining communities and one on which the preachers were able to play. But we are forced to conclude that people were open then to religious persuasion in a way that is less true of our own day. Religion, it seems, was in their veins even when they did not give it any outward expression; and powerful gospel preaching was capable of moving them very deeply. They seemed to understand its language and the imagery to which it referred. It was an age when heaven and hell, even if crudely understood, were very real in the hearts and minds of the people.

Wesley's main concern was to strike a chord in the hearts of individuals, and to challenge them to put themselves right with God. He tells us that this happened on his first visit to Plessey, and from a different source we happen to know the name of one of those who responded. This was a young man called William Hunter, not, in fact, a miner but the son of a farmer in the Plessey neighbourhood. He was fifteen at the time of Wesley's visit and at that time his older brothers seemed to be more affected by the preacher than he was. But a seed had been planted in William's heart and in due course, after hearing more of Wesley and other preachers, he became a Methodist, and later a travelling preacher himself.[5]

The more general results of Wesley's work at Plessey were striking. A Society was founded and within a dozen years or so Wesley was able to write of it as follows:[6]

> The Society of colliers here may be a pattern to all societies in England. No person ever misses his class; they have no jar of any kind among them; but with one heart and one mind provoke one another to love and good works.

It sounds idyllic but there is no reason to think that it was not true within the Methodist Society at that time. Of course, not all miners were Methodist and we must not fall into the temptation of identifying the Society with the whole village. Nevertheless the influence of the Methodists was felt outside the bounds of the Society and must have affected the community as a whole in all kinds of ways.

In many other pit communities Methodist Societies were established, chapels built and lives changed. As time went on the chapel fellowships, and all the other agencies associated with them, such as Sunday Schools, became powerful influences for improving and civilising life in the pit villages. And looking further ahead, into the nineteenth century, the chapels also produced a great many able men who were able to assume positions of leadership in the trade unions and co-operatives which were struggling into birth at that time. Such a result could never have entered John Wesley's mind and yet it proved to be a natural consequence of the work which he began.

Charles Wesley also worked in the pit villages and was inspired by the experience to write some of his hymns. One of these, he said specifically, was written 'after preaching to the Newcastle colliers'. It begins Ye neighbours and friends of Jesus drawn near.'[7] Another hymn written about the same time has as its opening lines, 'See how great a flame aspires', an image said to have been possibly suggested to the writer by the sight of the large colliery fires which illuminated the countryside on the darkest nights. Whether that is true or not, the hymn certainly conveys the excitement felt by the Wesleys as they saw their work bearing fruit even in the most inhospitable circumstances. It is worth hearing more of it:[8]

See how great a flame aspires
  Kindled by a spark of grace!
Jesu's love the nations fires,
  Sets the kingdoms on a blaze.
To bring fire on earth he came
  Kindled in some hearts it is:
O that all might catch the flame,
  All partake the glorious bliss!

When he first the work begun,
  Small and feeble was his day:
Now the word doth swiftly run,
  Now it wins its widening way;
More and more it spreads and grows
  Ever mighty to prevail;
Sin's strongholds it now o'erthrows,
  Shakes the trembling gates of hell.

The long-term effect of Methodism on the pit villages is well described by one of those miners' leaders mentioned at the beginning of this chapter, Jack Lawson:[9]

The Methodist Revival of the eighteenth century came to mining communities in the time of economic, social and moral chaos. The people were mazed and dazed by the greatest economic cataclysm in human history. The miners were almost its first and chief victims . . . Through these communities the mighty Revival suddenly swept, catching them in the swirl of its emotionalism, arousing new desires, enlarging the individual, searching out and steeling the will. The chapel was their first social centre. Here it was they drew together, found strength in their weakness, and expressed to each other their hidden thoughts and needs. The chapel gave them their first music, their first literature and philosophy to meet the harsh life and cruel impact of the crude materialistic age. Here men first found the language and art to express their antagonism to grim conditions and injustice.

Their hymns and sermons may have been of another world, but the first fighters and speakers for unions, Co-op societies, political freedom, and improved conditions were Methodist preachers. That is beyond argument.

REFERENCES

1. *See Jack Lawson, A Man's Life, 1932 and Peter Lee, 1949.*
2. *Journal iii, 68. Miners may have heard him in Newcastle on his first two visits. They certainly did on later visits.*
3. *Ibid., 68-69. A chapel was built on the Fell near Chowdene in 1754, though it no longer stands today.*
4. *Ibid., 73-74. On Plessey see an article by Dr. J. C. Bowmer in Bulletin 37 (March 1982) of the Wesley Historical Society, N.E. Branch.*
5. *See his life in E.M.P. ii, also Steele, pp.83-85.*
6. *Journal iv, 219-20.*
7. *First published in Charles Wesley's Hymns and Sacred Poems, 1749. The hymn is omitted from Hymns & Psalms, 1983.*
8. *Also published in Hymns and Sacred Poems, 1749. Number 781 in Hymns & Psalms.*
9. *A Man's Life, pp.110-11. The whole of chapter 10, entitled 'Little Bethel' is relevant and interesting. The relation of Methodism to mining communities in County Durham is closely analysed in Robert Moore, Pitmen, Preachers and Politics, 1974.*

V

MISUNDERSTANDING AND OPPOSITION

We have already noted a number of instances of opposition to the Methodist movement in its early years. The nature of opposition was varied – some of it was mindless, some malicious, some the result of religious prejudice or of conscientious disagreement. Much certainly was due to a misunderstanding of what John Wesley was trying to achieve, but it has to be admitted that some of those who opposed him thought they understood very well what he was about, and did not like it. One of the frequent charges against Methodism was that of expecting too much of human nature, leading to false piety and hypocrisy. This was an easy target for ridicule, a nice example of which is found in a farce performed in Newcastle in November 1743. The play-bill read:

> For the benefit of Mr. Este
> By the Edinburgh company of comedians,
> on Friday, November 4, will be acted a Comedy called
> THE CONSCIOUS LOVERS
> To which will be added a farce, called
> TRICK UPON TRICK, OR METHODISM DISPLAYED.

However, the first performance, as described in Wesley's Journal proved more alarming to the mockers than to the Methodists:[1]

> On Friday a vast multitude of spectators were assembled in the Moot Hall to see this. It was believed there could not be less than fifteen hundred people, some hundreds of whom sat on rows of seats built upon the stage. Soon after the comedians had begun the first act of the play, on a sudden all those seats fell down at once, the supporters of them breaking like a rotten stick. The people were thrown one upon another, about five foot forward, but not one of them hurt. After a short time the rest of the spectators were quiet, and the actors went on. In the middle of the second act all the shilling seats gave a crack and sunk several inches down. A great noise and shrieking followed; and as many as could readily get to the door went out and

returned no more. Notwithstanding this, when the noise was over, the actors went on with the play. In the beginning of the third act the entire stage suddenly sunk about six inches. The players retired with great precipitation; yet in a while they began again. At the latter end of the third act all the sixpenny seats, without any kind of notice, fell to the ground. There was now a cry on every side, it being supposed that many were crushed in pieces; but, upon inquiry, not a single person (such was the mercy of God!) was either killed or dangerously hurt. Two or three hundred remaining still in the hall, Mr Este (who was to act the Methodist) came upon the stage and told them, for all this, he was resolved the farce should be acted. While he was speaking the stage sunk six inches more; on which he ran back in the utmost confusion, and the people as fast as they could out of the door, none staying to look behind him.

Which is most surprising – that those players acted this farce the next week, or that some hundreds of people came again to see it?

The Wesleys obviously could not take the production of anti-Methodist farces very seriously. They must, however, have been grieved by the opposition they received from fellow clergymen and from ministers of Dissenting congregations, who they might have hoped would sympathise with their efforts to make Christianity vital and powerful among ordinary people. The trouble was that for various reasons many of these ministers did not like the Wesleys' methods or their manner. Dissenting ministers might show their displeasure by threatening to excommunicate any of their members who associated with the Methodists – this certainly happened in Newcastle and other places. Church of England parsons might take more drastic measures, using their social position to rouse active opposition to the Methodists. Let us hear Charles Wesley's journal for June 1743 for an instance of this:[2]

We rode to (South) Shields. I went to (St. Hilda's) church and the people flocked in crowds after me. The minister could not be heard in reading prayers; but I heard him loud enough afterward, calling for the Church wardens to quiet the disturbance which none but himself had raised. I fancy he thought I should preach there like some of the first Quakers. The clerk came to me, bawling out it was consecrated ground, and I had no business to preach on it; I was no minister etc. When he had cried himself out of breath, I whispered him in the ear that I had not intention to preach there; and he stumbled upon a good saying, 'Sir, if you have any word of exhortation for the people, speak it to them without'. I did so at my leisure, a huge multitude waiting in the churchyard; many of them fierce, and threatening to drown me, and what not. I walked quietly thro' the midst of them and discoursed in strong, awakening words, on the jailer's question 'What must I do to be saved?' The Churchwardens and others laboured in vain to interrupt, by throwing dirty hay, and money, among the people. Having delivered my message I rode to the ferry; crossed; and met as rough friends on the other side. The Mob of North Shields waited to salute me, with the Minister at their head. He had got a man with a horn, instead of a trumpet, and bade him blow and his companions shout. Others were almost as violent in their approbation. We went thro' honour and dishonour (but neither of them hurt us) and by 6 with God's blessing came safe to Newcastle.

Sometimes a Church of England parson was personally sympathetic to Methodism but was later persuaded to change his mind. Let us hear Charles Wesley again, describing a visit to Whickham in October 1746:[3]

The curate sent his love to me, with a message he was glad of my coming and obliged to me for endeavouring to do good among his people; for none wanted it more; and he heartily wished me good luck in the name of the Lord. He came with another clergyman and stayed both preaching and society. It was the exemplary behaviour of our society, with the deaths of two or three, which convinced the ministers that this new sect, everywhere spoken against, is no other than the sect of the Nazarenes or real Christians.

There was a different story two months later:[4]

I called upon Mr _ _ _ at Whickham, whose countenance was changed. He had been with the Bishop who forbade his conversing with me. I marvel the prohibition did not come sooner.

John Wesley had a similar experience at Osmotherley in 1747. On his journey northwards to Newcastle he arrived at Osmotherley on Sunday, 1st March:[5]

I came to Osmotherley about ten o-clock, just as the minister* (who lives some miles off) came into town. I sent my service to him, and told him, if he pleased, I would assist him, either by reading prayers or preaching. On receiving the message, he came to me immediately, and said he would willingly accept of my assistance. As we walked to church he said, 'Perhaps it would fatigue you too much to read prayers and preach too.' I told him no; I would choose it, if he pleased; which I did accordingly. After service was ended, Mr. D. said, 'Sir, I am sorry I have not an house here to entertain you. Pray let me know whenever you come this way.' Several asking where I would preach in the afternoon, one went to Mr. D. again, and asked if he was willing I should preach in the church. He said, 'Yes, whenever Mr. Wesley pleases.' We had a large congregation at three o'clock. Those who in times past had been the most bitter gainsayers seemed now to be melted into love. All were convinced we are no Papists. How wisely does God order all things in their season!

* Mr. Dyson.

Village centre, Osmotherley

Seven weeks later, when Wesley called at Osmotherley on his journey south there was a different story:[6]

About nine I preached to a large congregation at Renton* and before six reached Osmotherley. Finding Mr. D. (as I expected) had been vehemently attacked by the neighbouring clergy and gentry, that he might be exposed to no farther difficulty on my account I did not claim his promise, but preached on a tombstone near the church, on 'The Lord is risen indeed'. How wisely does God order all things! Some will not hear even the word of God out of a church; for the sake of these we are often permitted to preach in a church. Others will not hear it in a church: for their sakes we are often compelled to preach in the highways.

*Rainton, between Sunderland and Durham

Despite these disappointments it has to be admitted that some ministers of all denominations did view the Methodists sympathetically and co-operate with them. One such was Mr. T. Wardrobe, a Dissenting minister at Hexham, who invited Charles Wesley to that town in November 1746.[7] Charles arrived there on 27th November, the first visit there by either of the Wesley brothers. However, owing to the efforts of one or two local gentry his visit was a lively one:[8]

The only place I could get to preach was in the cockpit; and I expected Satan would come and fight me on his own ground. Squire Roberts, the justice's son, laboured hard to raise a mob, (for whose riot I was to answer) but with a strong hand did the Lord hold down him that is in the world. The very boys ran away from him when the poor Squire persuaded them to go down to the cockpit and cry 'Fire'. I called, in words then first heard in that place, 'Repent, and be converted, that your sins may be blotted out.' God struck the hard rock, and the water gushed out. Never have I seen a people more desirous at the first hearing. I passed the evening in conference with Mr. Wardrobe. O that all our dissenting brethren were like minded! Then would all dissensions cease for ever.

Charles was back at Hexham a few weeks later, and once again was able to turn the tables on his opponents:[9]

I rode to Hexham and preached, at the Cross, repentance towards God and faith in Jesus Christ. All opposition was kept down and the Lord was with us of a truth. At four I attempted to preach at the Cockpit. Satan resented it and sent, as his champions to maintain his cause, the two butlers of the two justices. They brought their cocks and set them a-fighting. I gave them the ground and walked straight to the cross, where we had four times as many as the other place could hold. Our enemies followed, and strove all the ways permitted them to annoy us. Neither their fireworks, nor their water works, could stop the course of the Gospel. I lifted up my voice like a trumpet, and many had ears to hear.

Talk of 'water works' was no idle metaphor. When John Wesley visited Barnard Castle in May 1752 the fire engine was hauled out to play water on the open-air congregation. A few loyal Methodists tried to intervene but were overpowered by the mob.[10] One of those Methodists was a young man of 18 called Thomas Hanby. In due course he felt called to preach himself, but for some time resisted the call because of the harsh treatment he had seen meted out at Barnard Castle to various Methodist preachers who had often stood preaching in the market-place with blood running down their faces as a result of blows, and of missiles thrown at them.[11]

I was truly miserable. I remembered the wormwood and the gall that the preachers drank at Barnard Castle; and I said in my heart, I will not preach.

He did become a travelling preacher, but as he had rightly anticipated he did have some hair-raising experiences with angry and besotted mobs in places like Leek and Burton-upon-Trent, when his actual life seemed to be in danger.

Christopher Hopper of Ryton, who has appeared earlier in this book, gives his own account of the opposition and enmity he faced when setting out on his preaching work:[12]

I met with great persecution, many discouragements, and much opposition in every place. Men of all ranks used their power and influence to stop this blessed work of God.

They spoke all manner of evil against the work, and the instruments employed therein. They dispensed with two or three awakened clergymen tolerably well: these were regularly ordained, men of learning, gentlemen, and divines but to see a ploughman, or an honest mechanic, stand up to preach the gospel, it was insufferable. Hell was moved from beneath; a council was called; the edict came forth, and war commenced.

Laymen and ecclesiastics joined heart and hand to suppress these pestilent fellows – not with acts of kindness, Scripture, or reason, but invectives and lies, dirt, rotten eggs, brickbats, stones, and cudgels: these were Satan's arguments in vindication of his own cause. It was the common cry in town and country, 'Press them for soldiers; send them on board a man-of-war; transport them; beat them; stone them; send them to prison, or knock out their brains and dispatch them at once; for there is no law for them.'

Several of my fellow sufferers had shared honest John Nelson's fate already; and I expected to be the next.

Some of the worst physical violence meted out to a preacher must be that suffered by John Nelson, the Yorkshire stone mason. Not only was he impressed as a soldier, as Hopper here reminds us, but he had some terrible experiences in his later travels on behalf of the Methodists. One particularly vicious attack on Nelson occurred on Easter Sunday, 1747 when he was preaching near York.

John Wesley met Nelson at Osmotherley the next day and heard his account of his sufferings which so impressed him that he put it into his journal.[13]

Towards the close of his discourse a mob came from York, hired and headed by some (miscalled) gentlemen. They stood still, till an eminent Papist cried out, 'Why do not you knock the dog's brains out?' On which they immediately began throwing all that came to hand, so that the congregation was quickly dispersed. John spoke a few words, and walked toward York. They followed with showers of bricks and stones, one of which struck him on the shoulder, one on the back, and, a little before he came to the city, part of a brick hit him on the back part of the head and felled him to the ground. When he came to himself two of Acomb lifted him up, and led him forward between them. The gentlemen followed, throwing as before, till he came to the city gate, near which lived an honest tradesman, who took him by the arm and pulled him into his house. Some of the rioters swore they would break all his windows if he did not turn him out. But he told them resolutely, 'I will not; and let any of you touch my house at your peril: I shall make you remember it as long as you live.' On this they thought good to retire.

After a surgeon had dressed the wound in his head, John went softly on to Acomb. About five he went out, in order to preach, and began singing a hymn. Before it was ended the same gentlemen came in a coach from York, with a numerous attendance. They threw clods and stones so fast on every side that the congregation soon dispersed. John walked down into a little ground not far from Thomas Slaton's house.

John Nelson

Two men quickly followed, one of whom swore desperately he would have his life. And he seemed to be in good earnest. He struck him several times, with all his force, on the head and breast; and at length threw him down and stamped upon him, till he left him for dead; but, by the mercy of God, being carried into a house, he soon came to himself; and, after a night's rest, was so recovered that he was able to ride to Osmotherley.

In the light of this kind of experience it is astounding that men were prepared to enter the ranks of Wesley's travelling preachers, and to risk reputation, limbs and life in the work, especially when the material rewards were so slight – little more than £20 a year for a married man plus subsistence. But their call came, they believed, from God and they were prepared to spend and be spent in a vocation whose spiritual importance outweighed all their personal sufferings and sacrifices.

REFERENCES

1. *Journal*, iii, 110-11.

2. *Life of C.W.*, i, 335.

3. *Ibid.*, 453.

4. *Ibid.*, 456.

5. *Journal*, iii, 283-84.

6. *Ibid.*, 290.

7. See Stamp, pp.79-81 for a letter from Wardrobe to John Wesley. See also *Journal* iii, 235, iv 116 n. and 164.

8. *Life of C.W.*, i, 456.

9. *Ibid.*

10. *Journal*, iv, 29. See the next reference also.

11. *E.M.P.*, ii, contains the account of Thomas Hanby's Life.

12. *E.M.P.*, i, 191-92.

13. *Journal*, iii, 290-91.

VI

JOHN WESLEY AND GRACE MURRAY

In the old parish registers of St. Andrew's Church, Newcastle upon Tyne, written in a beautiful clerical hand, can be found the following:

Weddings in October 1749

1st *Charles Plimmer and Ann Lemmon*
3rd *John Bennet and Grace Murray*
27th *Edmund Holmes and Sarah Thirsby*

How easy it is to regard register entries such as this simply as a catalogue of names and dates – how easy to forget that they refer to persons once as much alive as we are now and that behind the names there lies a human story, sometimes calm and placid, sometimes full of emotional cross-currents and misunderstandings. For the vast majority of the entries in the older registers this background detail is, of course, lost for ever, but for some we are able to find out enough to make the entries come alive in a very real way. This is certainly the case for the wedding recorded under the date 3rd October 1749 between John Bennet and Grace Murray; and in the story behind that event John Wesley had a very close and direct involvement since, if all had gone as he had hoped, it would have been his name and not John Bennet's which stood against that of Grace Murray in the St. Andrew's register. Let us try to unravel the story.[1]

John Wesley was 46 years old at the time we are speaking of. He had already spent a decade in the arduous work of a travelling preacher, and organiser of the Methodist Societies. He had endured all that English weather, English roads and English mobs could do to hinder or prevent his evangelistic work, yet he had seen it blossom and flower marvellously under what he firmly believed as the providence of God. He had done all this as a bachelor – indeed, one might almost say a convinced celibate. From his boyhood Wesley had, on his own confession, held an aversion to marriage, one major reason being:[2]

Because I should never find such a woman as my father had.

In this admission as in much else, we trace in John Wesley's character the influence and example of his remarkable mother, Susanna Wesley. But in his adult life and preacher work, other considerations had also weighed against the idea of matrimony – biblical injunctions, puritanical scruples, the need to preserve his freedom of movement as an evangelist, his reluctance to take on the expense of maintaining a wife and family, and so forth. John Wesley believed all this to be applicable not only to himself but also to his brother and those other preachers who were enlisted into the work; and they all had a working rule that none should enter into matrimony without consulting with and gaining the agreement of the others.

Yet, John Wesley was flesh and blood like any other man. Behind what often seems a composed, self-sufficient and even at times an arrogant exterior, there was a sensitive and affectionate nature, and one moreover which was undoubtedly susceptible to feminine charms. There is no doubt also that Wesley was attractive to women, and in the course of his work for Methodism he became acquainted with very many, often in situations of religious warmth and emotion where feelings might run unnaturally deep and words be misunderstood. By a mixture of self-control, ingenuousness and, it must be admitted, constantly keeping on the move, he managed to preserve his bachelordom! But by his mid-40s he was revising his views about marriage and looking for a possible partner. It so happened that he did not have to look very far. Grace Murray was a widow some dozen years younger than Wesley. While living in London she had been converted and became a very active Methodist, acquainted with both the Wesley brothers. In 1742 she returned to her native Newcastle and was soon fully engaged there in Methodist work associated with the Orphan House. Let us hear part of her own account:[3]

The (Methodist) society at Newcastle was divided into classes with their respective leaders, like those in London. Mr. Wesley fixed me in that part of the work which he thought proper; and when the House was finished, I was appointed to be the Housekeeper. Soon also the people were again divided into bands, or small select Societies, women by themselves and the men in like manner. I had a full hundred in classes, whom I met in two separate meetings, and a band for each day of the week. I likewise visited the sick and backsliders, which was my pleasant meat. The work of God was my delight, and when I was not employed in it, I seemed out of my element. We had also several Societies in the country, which I regularly visited, meeting the women in the daytime, and in the evening the whole Society. And oh! what pourings out of the Spirit have I seen at those times! It warms my heart now, while I relate it. I doubt not but I shall meet some of those precious souls, amongst whom I was so often refreshed in prayer, to sing the high praises of God and the Lamb for ever.

Grace was not a preacher but the extent of her duties and responsibilities reveals in an interesting way what scope there was for a woman of talent and dedication in early Methodism. It is hard to imagine any other religious group, apart from the Quakers, in which such openings for women's work could be found at that time. Many of her responsibilities were domestic and managerial, superintending the running of the Orphan House itself, including the oversight of the little residential community there, looking after the interests of the travelling preachers, and nursing those who were sick including, as we shall see, both John Wesley and John Bennet. But over and above this work Grace was entrusted with demanding and important pastoral and spiritual duties. In all this work her competence, her energy and her character are clearly evidenced. She seems to have combined masculine independence with feminine grace. Listen to this description of her mounting her horse:[4]

An old man once told how he saw her take leave at a house door in Yorkshire. Her horse stood waiting. She came out. A glance of her eye quickly told her all was right. No man might touch, even to help her, for she was on God's errand: so she laid her hand upon the conscious beast, and it knelt to receive her. She sprang lightly into the saddle, waved her arm, and as in a moment, was out of sight; and the old man saw her no more – except in dreams.

It is not surprising that men adored Grace Murray – nor that women were jealous of her! We can sense the feline undertones in this letter written to John Wesley in November 1748 by Jeannie Keith, a resident at the Orphan House and a close acquaintance of Grace:[5]

I know of nothing amiss between Sister Murray and me; but we cannot be of one soul as you express it; for you know she must have a little pre-eminence. I am exceeding willing that she should; and so we live in great peace, and I believe, in love . . . With God in my sight and heaven in my soul I think myself one of the happiest creatures below the skies. I do not complain that God has not made me some fine thing to be set up to be gazed at: but I can heartily bless Him that He has made me just as I am.

More open and strong things were said than that about Grace Murray – but not, of course, to Wesley. Some of the ill-feeling was due to petty envy, and some to elements in Grace's character, but much of it was caused by the special relationship she enjoyed with Wesley, who not only employed her fully in pastoral work but began to take her out with him on extended journeys to various parts of the country, and, in the autumn of 1748, to Ireland. These long and lonely journeys of Grace and John Wesley together really set the tongues wagging at Newcastle and elsewhere, and the darkest conclusions were drawn by some. John Wesley was well aware of all this but believed the innuendoes could be disregarded. He was sure Grace was meant for him and would be an ideal partner in his life's work. He had finally come to this conclusion while Grace was nursing him through a bout of illness at Newcastle in August 1748:[6]

I observed her narrowly both as to her temper, sense and behaviour. I esteemed and loved her more and more; and when I was a little recovered, I told her, sliding into it I know not how, 'If I ever marry I think you will be the person.' She was amazed and said, 'This is all I could ever have wished for under the sun – if I had <u>dared</u> to wish for it'.

Later on, in order to clear his own mind and to assure himself of the rightness of his decision, Wesley itemised for himself Grace's virtues in a list of points which emphasised her practical qualities and her potential usefulness to himself and the work of God. It was only on these grounds that he could justify marriage; the natural ties of affection on their own were not enough. In fact the word love never occurs in his list at all. Here are some points from it:

First, as a housekeeper she has every qualification I desire. She is remarkably neat in person, in clothes, in all things. She is nicely frugal, yet not sordid.

As a nurse (which my poor shattered, enfeebled carcass now frequently stands in need of) she is careful to the last degree, indefatigably patient and inexpressibly tender . . . she understands my constitution better than most physicians.

As a companion she has good sense and some knowledge both of men and books. She is of engaging temper and of a mild, sprightly, cheerful and yet serious nature.

As a friend she has been long tried and found faithful.

Lastly, as a fellow labourer in the Gospel of Christ (the light wherein my wife is to be chiefly considered) she has in a measure which I never found in any other both grace and gifts and fruit.

Wesley went on to add in a frank and revealing passage:[7]

She is and would be a continual defence (under God) against unholy desires and inordinate affections which I never did entirely conquer for six months together. She would likewise remove many hindrances from others, women in particular. She would guard many from inordinate affection for me, to which they would be far less exposed.

This is altogether a utilitarian catalogue of virtues but I don't think that there is any doubt that Wesley held Grace in the highest regard, or that had she become his wife, he would have offered her the fullest loyalty and affection. The truth was that, given the nature of his work, which he had no intention of giving up, he needed a wife who would offer the greatest interest and participation in it, and who would not impede but actually enhance his own usefulness. These qualities were more important to him than class, wealth or social graces. It is to John Wesley's credit that, though he could have chosen a gentlewoman, he had instead opted for a woman from the lower orders of society whose qualities he had tested and whom he deeply admired.

What, then, went wrong? It is easy to blame two men. One was John Bennet, one of Wesley's travelling preachers, a man of education and ability. Like Wesley but two years earlier, he had been nursed back to health (he thought from the grave) by Grace Murray and had concluded that God meant her to be his. A close relationship sprang up between the two and there was a very real understanding that they might marry. The second man who ruined John Wesley's hopes of marrying Grace was his own brother Charles. Charles had himself married a well-to-do heiress, Sarah Gwynne, in February 1749. But as soon as he heard from his brother in September of that year of his intention to marry Grace, he took immediate action to prevent it. He left John in Whitehaven where the two had met and rode to Hindley Hill farm in Allendale where Grace was staying – some of the old farm buildings still survive here. At Hindley Hill Charles' impetuosity swept all before it – he convinced Grace that the proposed marriage to John would be a disaster for Methodism, swept her off to Newcastle and there persuaded her and John Bennet to become man and wife without delay, presumably under a specially obtained licence as this all happened within a matter of days. Charles' high-handed action has been the subject of criticism ever since. What were his motives?

First (and ignobly) he certainly considered Grace as too low-born for his brother. Secondly (and perhaps with some justification) he misunderstood John's relationship with Grace and believed, or was persuaded by others to believe, that John was snatching her from Bennet whom Charles thought her lawful fiancé. Thirdly, he was acutely aware of the jealousy against Grace in some quarters,[8] and there were those in Newcastle very eager to add fuel to this particular conviction, not least Jane Keen who swore Mr. Wesley loved Grace 'beyond all sense and reason and that all the town was in an uproar and all the societies ready to fall in pieces'. This was related to the fourth conviction which moved Charles and which was indeed the major factor in his mind – namely a fear that the marriage would end John Wesley's effective leadership of the Methodist movement and that the great work of God would be broken up.

The only known portrait of Grace Murray, painted in old age.

Mary Vazeille, the Huguenot widow whom John Wesley married in 1751. She is holding a locket with what appears to be Wesley's portrait on it.

Charles' extraordinary course of action was therefore the result of profoundly held convictions and anxieties. Nevertheless he must be seen as the main agent in destroying his brother's hopes of marrying Grace. But Grace and John Wesley himself must bear some of the responsibility. For some considerable time Grace had veered indecisively between John Wesley and John Bennet. Both wanted to marry her and it seems that she simply couldn't or wouldn't make her mind up. I tend to think she really wanted Wesley but was conscious of all the implications and maybe could not quite believe that he really would make her his wife. One Methodist historian, writing over a hundred years ago dismissed Grace as a flirt.[9] This seems too severe a judgement, and unfair to Grace who obviously had admirable qualities, but it does remain true that she kept the hopes of both men alive, keeping her options open as we would call it.

John Wesley also was surely at fault for not being more positive and decisive at crucial moments. If he had really wanted Grace he could have had her. But his inner scruples held him back; perhaps we can trace his mother's influence here. Moreover he came to the conclusion, after Charles had taken Grace away, that he should not pursue them. He felt the choice now was between marriage and the work of God – and for him there was no question which had priority. On that fundamental point he and Charles were agreed, but the whole affair did create a serious if temporary rift between them.

There is little doubt that the loss of Grace was traumatic for John Wesley. We see this in a poem he wrote describing his feelings at the time – an unusual piece of writing for him in which he bares his soul and shows the vulnerable depths within. It is a long poem. The first 27 stanzas speak of Grace, and of their love and companionship. But then:[10]

> *Such was the friend, than life more dear,*
> *Whom in one luckless, baleful hour*
> *(For ever mentioned with a tear)*
> *The tempest's unresisted power*
> *(Oh, the unutterable smart!)*
> *Tore from my inly-bleeding heart.*

> *Unsearchable Thy judgements are,*
> *O Lord, a bottomless abyss!*
> *Yet sure, Thy love, Thy guardian care*
> *O'er all Thy works extended is:*
> *Oh! why didst Thou the blessing send?*
> *Or why thus snatch away my friend?*

Those verses were written on horseback riding to Newcastle from Leeds. At Leeds John had met his brother Charles, and Grace and her new husband, a day or two after the wedding. After some scenes of powerful emotion there was, largely thanks to John Wesley, a general reconciliation. He then rode without delay to Newcastle to pick up the threads of his work again there, despite the fact that his name in that town was currently mud, owing to all the misunderstanding and rumour in connection with himself and Grace. After that he accepted an invitation to undertake some difficult evangelical work at Rochdale on behalf of the very man who had taken Grace from him – John Bennet. Whatever we think of John Wesley it is impossible to deny his courage and magnanimity.

Whether Grace would have proved an ideal partner for him we shall never know. What we do sadly know is that when he finally did marry Mrs. Mary Vazeille in 1751 he made a big mistake and the union was disastrous.[11] It seems that John Wesley was not destined to know married bliss or the comforts of a family home.

Despite the pain this undoubtedly caused him he was able at last to take a philosophical (or should we say theological) viewpoint, as recorded by his friend, confidant and biographer, the Irish-born preacher Henry Moore:[12]

> He believed the Lord overruled this painful business for good, and that, if Mrs. Wesley had been a better wife, he might have been unfaithful to the great work to which God had called him, and might have too much sought to please her according to her own views.

REFERENCES

1. *There are a good many accounts of the Grace Murray episode, each throwing light on particular aspects. See for instance Stamp, pp.43-54, and also pp. 277-83 where Wesley's poem on Grace is given in full; Jackson's account in his* Life of Charles Wesley, *vol. (i), pp.535-41;* Journal, *iii, 427-40 with extensive annotations; Tyerman, ii, 42-57, and Ayling, Chapter 10. Wesley wrote his own account of the affair which is naturally the most illuminating of all. It was published in 1848 (edited by C. Hook) under the title* Narrative of a remarkable transaction in the early life of John Wesley, *and is referred to in the footnotes below as* Narrative. *See also G. Elsie Harrison* Son to Susanna *1937 (Penguin edit. 1944) esp. chapters 22-31. Though somewhat romanticised this is well founded on sources and gives a lively and perceptive insight into early Methodism, and John Wesley's relations with Grace.*

2. *Narrative, p.35.*

3. *Stamp, pp.47-48.*

4. *Ibid., p.49.*

5. *Ibid., pp.86-88.*

6. *Narrative, p.9.*

7. *Ibid., pp.35-38, compare this with S.C. Carpenter's comment on Wesley: 'There was no sex-side in his character'!* Eighteenth Century Church and People, *1959, p.209.*

8. *The strength of feeling among the London Methodists is indicated by the following: 'Some commotion was caused amongst the members at*

the Foundery (i.e. the Methodist preaching house and meeting place in London) by the presence there of Grace Murray who was hoping to become Mr. Wesley's wife. She was plainly advised to give up all such thoughts, as the London society thought her an unsuitable person, and consequently she would not be likely to meet with that respect from them as would be due to Mr. Wesley's wife.' G. J. Stevenson, City Road Chapel, London, and its associations, 1872, p.43.

9. L. Tyerman, Life and Times of the Rev. John Wesley, 2nd edition 1872, vol. ii, p.55.

10. Stamp, p.283. The poem of 31 verses was originally printed in Wesley's Narrative.

11. The following entry in Wesley's Journal under 2 Feb. 1751 is interesting: 'Having received full answer from Mr. Vincent Perronet, I was clearly convinced that I ought to marry. For many years I remained single because I believed I could be more useful in a single than in a married state. And I praise God who enabled me to do so. I now as fully believed that in my present circumstances I might be more useful in a married state; into which, upon this clear conviction, and by the advice of my friends, I entered a few days after.' (Journal iii, 512.) This is the only mention of the actual marriage in the Journal, over two weeks before it actually took place. (We have to remember that the Journal was written up periodically, not as a daily account.) There are some vivid descriptions of Wesley's relations with his wife in Jackson's Life of Charles Wesley, i, 565-71; Hampson, ii, 123-28 etc.

12. Stanley Ayling, John Wesley 1979, p.231.

VII

EARLY METHODISM IN SUNDERLAND

The pioneer of Methodism in Sunderland was Charles Wesley. In the course of his second north-eastern tour he rode over from Newcastle on 16th June 1743 to preach the first Methodist sermon on Wearside. He admitted in his journal that he had, for some reason (maybe just weariness), a strong aversion to preaching on this occasion, but he set his feelings aside as best he could and went ahead:[1]

> I dragged myself to about a thousand wild people and cried – 'O Israel, thou hast destroyed thyself, but in me is thy help.' Never have I seen greater attention in any at their first hearing.

When Charles describes the people who turned out to hear him as 'wild' he may mean that they were poorly dressed, or that they looked amazed at his preaching – or both. He obviously was not referring to their behaviour as they seem to have been surprisingly attentive. Not all preachers got away so lightly in Sunderland. Christopher Hopper of Ryton had to endure more than his fair share of opposition in Sunderland as in other places:[2]

> I did not much regard a little dirt, a few rotten eggs, the sound of a cow's horn, the noise of bells, or a few snowballs in their season. But sometimes I was saluted with blows, stones, brickbats and bludgeons . . . I sometimes lost a little skin and once a little blood which was drawn from my forehead by a sharp stone.

This wounding was the result of being pelted by a crowd of hooligan Sunderland sailors, probably drunk at the time. However, it has to be admitted that records of the ill treatment of preachers at Sunderland are few. This may be partly explained by the nature of the town. As with many sea ports it was an open, tolerant community, with a frank, outspoken and democratic air about it. It wasn't dominated by parsons and squires. In the seventeenth century it had been a strongly puritan town. One result of this was that two of its parish churches, Sunderland and Monkwearmouth, were low church or evangelical in Wesley's day; another result was that Sunderland had a strong nonconformist tradition. All this helped to create a favourable context for Methodism which took ready root, and right from the start found in Sunderland some staunch supporters who were willing to stand up for the movement and give it their protection. There is a nice example of this on the occasion of John Wesley's first visit, about a month after that of Charles, on 11th July 1743. The crowd who were listening to him became restive and noisy, and one or two missiles were thrown. Then, or so the story goes:

A big burly fishwife put her arms round the preacher's neck, shook her fist at the crowd, and cried in broad Sunderland: 'If any yan o' ye lifts up another hand to touch ma canny man, aal floor 'e dereckerly!'

The threat sufficed! Wesley was allowed to carry on. The story is apocryphal but has the ring of truth.

Holy Trinity (the parish church of Sunderland) erected in 1719. Wesley worshipped here, and preached in the nearby daughter church of St. John's, built in 1769.

John Wesley took his stand on that occasion, as Charles no doubt had a few weeks earlier, in High Street, probably standing near or actually on the old market cross.[3] This was in the heart of old Sunderland, the area which is now the far east end of the modern town.   At that time it was a lively industrial and commercial community, running parallel to the River Wear which was busy with sailing ships and keel boats. High Street served both as the main thoroughfare and the market; on either side of the street were the old large houses of the merchants and also many shops, and off High Street ran a complex of lanes and courts where the rapidly growing population were building their hopes. The fine brick-built parish church set back from High Street near the town moor, dated from 1719; a large daughter church was to be built in 1769, St. John's.

There were meeting houses for Quakers, Presbyterians, Baptists and others. Across the river was Monkwearmouth with its ancient church of St. Peter's and half a mile to the west was Bishopwearmouth, a separate rural community at that time, gathered round another old church, St. Michael's. John Wesley's activities on Wearside appear to have been associated either with the east end community of Sunderland, or with Monkwearmouth over the river, not with Bishopwearmouth which he never mentions in his journal.   However, he must have passed through Bishopwearmouth since the road from Sunderland to Newcastle went through that village, on its way to South Hylton where travellers crossed the River Wear by ford or ferry in the days before the first Wear bridge was built in Sunderland, several years after Wesley died.

It was somewhere along that road to Newcastle that Charles Wesley, accompanied by his wife and some friends, was travelling from Sunderland in August 1751 when he had an unusual experience which he recorded in his journal:[4]

At nine we set out and in half an hour's riding overtook a woman and a girl leading a horse. She begged us to help them and forward them on their way. We did so – but the horse turned with them again and rode back towards Sunderland. We had the riders to pick up again and remount. Their horse we put between us; but he broke thro' a gap and galloped back. When he had shaken them he stood still. I bade my companion take up the girl behind him, hoping the horse would carry the woman along; but in vain; though we all beat the poor beast to drive him on he kicked and flounced till he had dismissed his rider. I then said, 'Surely good woman, God withstands you. You are going somewhere contrary to his will. I can compare your horse to nothing but Balaam's ass; what can be the meaning of it?' She answered 'Sir, I will tell you all; for there must be something extra-ordinary in the great pains you have taken with me. That child I had by a gentleman who promised me marriage, but (has) since married another, because richer than I. I am going to try (to see) if he will do anything for the child and me; but I fear it is not pleasing to God.' I asked what she had to live upon. She told me she was married to a blacksmith, had a child by him, and it was but low with them. I advised her to take God's warning, and utterly renounce the first wicked man; to spend the rest of her days in repentance, and working out her salvation; gave her something; and recommended her to a sister in Sunderland. She seemed overwhelmed with joy and gratitude, mounted with her child, and the horse carried them quietly home.

This is an interesting story which shows the delight taken by the Wesleys in any inexplicable happenings which might be shown to have a supernatural meaning. Such occasions could be used to reinforce their conviction of the reality of the spiritual world, and of the hand of God in all things. In this respect John Wesley was more credulous than his brother, and was ready to take seriously all kinds of stories of paranormal and ghostly happenings – we shall come to an example a little later on.

That episode of the woman and the horse took place after Charles Wesley's third and last visit to Sunderland. By contrast his brother John was to visit the town over 30 times between 1743 and 1790 and hence must be regarded as the major inspirer and architect of Sunderland Methodism.

Even so we must always remember the contribution of others – Methodism was never simply a one-man show, dependent on John Wesley alone. Much of the patient building was done by other men and women including the travelling preachers appointed by Wesley to serve in the north-east. One of the earliest of these was the ex-stone mason John Nelson. He became known in Sunderland when awaiting release from his impressment into the army, and made such an impression with his preaching that he was soon invited back:[5]

> *When I was at London, I received a letter from Sunderland, wherein I was desired to go and preach there. Two men who had conversed with me when I was captive there had found the Lord; and they said that their souls panted for the salvation of their neighbours. So I see that God leads the blind by a way they know not; for I thought all that I had said there was as water spilt on the ground . . .*
>
> *Soon after I went to Newcastle, and laboured there about three months, and had an opportunity to visit Sunderland. I preached at the Cross to the greatest part of the town, who behaved well, and stood all the time, though the snow was eight or nine inches deep. I went there as often as I could; and God visited many with His salvation there, and at Painshaw and Biddick, who blessed God that I had been sent among them. They said that they would pray for our minister, who was the cause of my coming; for they were more beholden to him than to me; and, let him intend what he would, they had reason to bless God in his behalf. So it is evident God hath His way in the whirlwind, and His path in the great waters.*

The minister the Methodists of Sunderland were praying for was the parson of Nelson's home parish who was one of those most responsible for having had him unjustly impressed into the army. Without that, Nelson might never have gone to Sunderland at all and they might not have become Methodists – so they were happy to rejoice that God moves in mysterious ways.

It may have been under Nelson that a Methodist Society was established in Sunderland; it grew to 100 members by about 1750 and to 370 by the later 1770s. These are the numbers of the ticket-holding members – the 'hard core', we might say. Very many more than these would attend Methodist worship or hear the preacher in the open air, but it was the Society members who were expected to uphold the strict principles of Methodism. John Wesley on his visit in 1752 appeared to think well of them:[6]

I rode to Sunderland, where I found one of the liveliest societies in the north of England. This is the effect of their being so much 'under the law' as to scruple, one and all, the buying even of milk on a Sunday. The house hardly contained the people at five the next morning.

But Wesley's estimation of the Methodists in Sunderland was tainted by one particular weakness of theirs – smuggling. Smuggling was almost a way of life in coastal towns and was obviously not regarded by most folk as incompatible with being a Christian. We find the following entry for instance in the vivid diary of the country parson, James Woodforde, a younger contemporary of Wesley and Rector of Weston Longeville in Norfolk:[7]

March 29th 1777: Andrews the Smuggler brought me this night about 11 o'clock a bag of Hyson Tea, 6 pound weight. He frightened us a little by whistling under the parlour window just as we were going to bed. I gave him some Geneva and paid him for the tea at 10/6 per pound.

Wesley had a different standard. In his Rules for the Societies published first in Newcastle in 1743 he had stated that members should avoid evil of every kind, 'especially that which is most generally practised; and the examples given by Wesley included 'buying and selling uncustomed goods'. In Wesley's eyes this was a double dishonesty – to God and the king. Something therefore had to be done with the Sunderland Methodists:[8]

Thursday 16th June 1757: In the evening I preached at Sunderland. I then met the society, and told them plain none could stay with us unless he would part with all sin – particularly, robbing the King; selling or buying run goods, which I could no more suffer than robbing on the highway. This I enforced on every member the next day. A few would not promise to refrain, so these I forced to cut off. About two hundred and fifty were of a better mind.

Two years later he refers to the matter again:

Saturday, 23rd June 1759: I spoke to each of the society in Sunderland. Most of the robbers, commonly called smugglers, have left us; but more than twice the number of honest people are already come in their place. And if none had come, yet should I not dare to keep those who steal either from the King or subject.

Even then it is doubtful if he had got to the bottom of the business. Eighteen years later in 1777 we find him making this significant entry:[9]

Saturday 3rd May: I went to Sunderland, and strongly enforced 'Render unto Caesar the things that are Caesar's.'

By this time the Sunderland Society had its own purpose-built preaching house, on Numbers Garth, built in 1759 off High Street, just behind the old Quaker meeting house of that period. No trace of either of these buildings survives today and even the successor of the Numbers Garth chapel, built on the corner of Sans Street in 1793, has been demolished. This big chapel had been much rebuilt though did preserve the old original datestone. The loss of these old buildings, and indeed the virtual destruction of old Sunderland as Wesley knew it, makes it hard for us today to recreate, except in imagination, the physical context of his work on Wearside. One or two things, however, have survived. Holy Trinity Church, the parish church of Sunderland, for instance, still stands. Wesley occasionally worshipped here, as on Trinity Sunday 1755:[10]

Sunday 25th May: I preached at eight, though not without pain, not having recovered my voice. We had a useful sermon at church. As soon as the sacrament was over I preached in the High Street (it being Trinity Sunday), upon 'There are three that bear record in heaven'; and my voice was so restored that I could command the whole congregation, though it was exceeding large.

This brief entry reminds us of the Church of England connection strongly maintained by Wesley – and expected of the Methodists also. Some Sunderland Methodists took this very seriously and it was not until thirty years after Wesley died that the big Sans Street chapel ceased to hold its services at times different from the parish church, a practice which had allowed those who wished to attend both chapel and church.

*The Sans Street Wesleyan Chapel, Sunderland, built 1793,
two years after Wesley's death.*

Another physical link with the age of Wesley is St. Peter's Church, Monkwearmouth. As has already been said this was a church with a puritan tradition and the Perpetual Curate in Wesley's time, Thomas Goodday, was a friend of Wesley and approved of his work, as did his successor Jonathan Ivison. This must have been a very refreshing change from the coolness, suspicion, or downright opposition of some parsons in other places. During his visits to Sunderland, Wesley preached at least 15 times at St. Peter's, and occasionally conducted worship there also. Of course, as well as preaching here by invitation, he also led worship in the Methodist fashion in other places in Monkwearmouth – especially at the large Wesleyan chapel built there on Whitburn Street in 1761.

Let us turn to a subject that took Wesley's interest on his visit to Sunderland in 1768:[11]

> *Wednesday the 25th May and the two following days, being at Sunderland, I took down, from one who had feared God from her infancy, one of the strangest accounts I ever read; and yet I can find no pretence to disbelieve it. The well-known character of the person excludes all suspicion of fraud; and the nature of the circumstances themselves excludes the possibility of a delusion.*

The person referred to was Elizabeth Hobson, a young woman of 22 who was apparently a Methodist. She was reluctant to divulge her story to Wesley but eventually did so and he recorded it in detail and at great length in his journal. From childhood Elizabeth Hobson had had very acute psychic powers, having, so she alleged, frequent visions of persons, usually around the time of their deaths. Not surprisingly in Sunderland these included visions of men drowned at sea:

> *John Simpson, one of our neighbours, a man that truly feared God, and one with whom I was particularly acquainted, went to sea, as usual. He sailed out on a Tuesday. The Friday night following, between eleven and twelve o'clock, I heard one walking in my room; and every step sounded as if he was stepping in water. He then came to the bedside, in his sea-jacket, all wet, and stretched his hand over me. Three drops of water fell on my breast, and felt as cold as ice. I strove to wake his wife, who lay with me; but I could not, any more than if she was dead. Afterward I heard he was cast away that night. In less than a minute he went away; but he came to me every night, for six or seven nights following, between eleven and two. Before he came and when he went away, I always heard sweet music.*

The climax to Elizabeth's tale concerned a persistent haunting by her dead grandfather, and the final laying of the ghost after a meeting with him on Boyldon Hill, or Building Hill as it became known, part of Sunderland's Mowbray Park today. Elizabeth's story is a very strange one. It includes a good many details of life in the town in her day which have an authentic ring, but the visions are very hard to understand. Wesley, however, gave the story full credence, and gives us his reasons, which were, in brief, that to give up belief in the spiritual dimension was to give up the basis of Christianity. In order not to concede any ground to atheists and materialists Wesley was prepared to go to the very limits of credulity:[12]

> *The English in general, and indeed most of the men of learning in Europe, have given up all accounts of witches and apparitions, as mere old wives' fables. I am sorry for it . . . The giving up witchcraft is in effect giving up the Bible.*

About 20 years later Wesley heard and was prepared to believe another strange young woman, Margaret Barlow of Darlington. Her visions were not of ghosts but of angels, and she stirred up considerable frenzy with prophecies of the imminent end of the world. The credence Wesley was prepared to give to this sort of thing was often a puzzle and a cause of anxiety to the sober and sensible Methodists in the north-east.[13] The eighteenth century is often called the age of reason. But superstition was certainly not dead. John Wesley seems to embody both the clear reason and the superstition of that age, but it's beyond argument that for him both reason and superstition were subservient to his profound Christian convictions.

We can end this survey of his work in Sunderland on a different note by holding in our minds a few vignettes from his later visits to the town. On a warm June evening in 1770, for instance, when four boat-loads of Methodist folk who had been with Wesley to a meeting in Biddick came sailing home down the river, singing their hymns and filling the valley of the Wear with the sound. Or of a Sunday in June 1788 when Wesley accepted an invitation from one of his former preachers, John Hampson, now Curate of St. John's Church, to preach in his church, and moved the congregation not only by his sermons but by the sight of the frail and venerable old prophet, walking down the aisle leaning on Hampson's arm. Or of another Sunday in 1790, when Wesley, nearly 87 and on his final visit to Wearside, preached a charity sermon in the morning at Monkwearmouth on behalf of the Sunday Schools (which he had done so much to encourage) and then later in the day preached in the open air on the Pann Fields to an audience of several thousand. Wesley must have known he would not see Sunderland again, but he had the satisfaction of knowing that Methodism was thriving in the town, and in the large Methodist Circuit covering much of northern Durham of which Sunderland was the head. In looking back over all his work in the town he could with justice exclaim on that day – 'Here it is plain, our labour has not been in vain!'[14]

REFERENCES

1. *Life of C.W.*, i, 335-56.

2. *E.M.P.*, i, 197.

3. *Wesley's visits to Sunderland and Monkwearmouth were recounted by the late Revd. F. F. Bretherton – see bibliography for details. The physical appearance of Sunderland in Wesley's day is vividly portrayed in John Rain's Eye Plan of Sunderland and Bishopwearmouth dated c.1785-90. The plan has been published in A4 sections, edited by Michael Clay, Geoffrey Milburn and Stuart Miller (1984).*

4. *Life of C.W.*, i, 580-81.

5. *E.M.P.*, i, 141-43.

6. *Journal*, iv, 24.

7. *James Woodforde, The Diary of a Country Parson, 1758-1802, ed., J. Beresford (1978), p.131.*

8. *Journal*, iv, 325.

9. *Journal*, iv, 144.

10. *Journal*, iv, 116.

11. *Elizabeth Hobson's story is found in Wesley's Journal, v, 265-75.*

12. *Ibid.*, 265.

13. *Ibid.*, vii, 398 and note. See also Steele, chapter 12.

14. *Ibid.*, viii, 72.

VIII

JOHN WESLEY IN NORTHUMBERLAND

One of my favourite paintings is a water colour in the Laing Gallery, Newcastle, of the old medieval bridge at Morpeth, painted in 1802 by the English artist Thomas Girtin who was to die tragically at the age of 27 that same year. Though the skies are threatening, the scene as a whole breathes an air of old-world, almost medieval tranquillity, and indeed the main feature shown, the bridge itself, dated from the thirteenth century. Picturesque though it certainly was, the bridge's age posed some problems:[1]

> It is extremely narrow, and so steep as to be very difficult in the ascent, and not less dangerous in the descent, especially to heavy-laden waggons. Both to people on foot and horseback the passage is equally inconvenient and perilous.

That was Eneas Mackenzie writing in the 1820s. He went on to drop a broad hint that the bridge urgently needed rebuilding, and whether or not his words were responsible, a new bridge was in fact built a few years later. Only a fragment of the old bridge now remains, but as we look at it today we may recall that it was over it that John Wesley rode on Monday 18th July 1748 on his first major tour of the eastern and northern parts of Northumberland.

This tour was made during Wesley's twelfth visit to the north-east, six years after his first arrival in 1742. During those six years his prime concern had been to establish Methodism in Newcastle and the Tyne-Wear area, and the farthest north he had travelled from Newcastle was to visit his beloved Methodist Society at the colliery village of Plessey near the River Blyth. What had made him decide to venture further north in 1748? Obviously there was a natural desire to extend his mission. Indeed, the word of Methodism had run ahead of Wesley into parts of Northumberland he had not yet been to, carried there by Northumbrian men and women who had heard Wesley in Newcastle or elsewhere, and had become Methodists themselves. Naturally they wanted Wesley to visit their home towns and to encourage the Societies they were endeavouring to found. This lay initiative was an important factor in Northumbrian Methodism, as indeed elsewhere, and serves as a useful reminder that the pioneering work was not all done by Wesley himself. In Alnwick, for instance, the first preacher was apparently John Trembath; and Robert Sutty had formed a society at Berwick before Wesley's arrival there. But we are jumping ahead – let's first hear Wesley's account of his arrival in Morpeth, which, as he makes plain in the first sentence, was not unexpected:[2]

> *Monday 18th July (1748): I began my journey northward, having been appointed to preach in Morpeth at noon. As soon as I had sung a few verses at the Cross, a young man appeared at the head of his troop, and told me, very plainly and roughly, 'You shall not preach there.' I went on; upon which he gave the signal to his companions who prepared to force me into better manners; but they quickly fell out among themselves. Meantime I began my sermon, and went on without any considerable interruption, the congregation softening more and more, till, toward the close, the far greater part appeared exceeding serious and attentive.*

The Cross at Morpeth was about 50 years old at that time, and was in a central position in the market-place near the town centre, forming an admirable open-air pulpit.   The attempt to prevent Wesley from preaching was obviously prearranged, but fizzled out very quickly. In fact there was little overt opposition to Methodism in Northumberland.   A dozen years later when Wesley was again preaching in Morpeth market-place, 'a few of the hearers were a little ludicrous at first – but their mirth was quickly spoiled'. This was very mild stuff compared to examples of persecution further south, and indicates a high degree of religious tolerance in Northumberland, though paradoxically this does not mean that Methodism was to take strong root in the county, as we shall see.

Let us continue with Wesley, on this first visit.   From Morpeth he rode to Widdrington, some nine miles north-east and towards the sea, a little working-class community with a tiny colliery nearby.[3]

> *In the afternoon we rode to Widdrington, which belonged to the Lord Widdrington till the Rebellion in 1715. The people flocked in from all parts, so that the congregation here was larger than at Morpeth. It was a delightful evening, and a*

delightful place, under the shade of tall trees. And every man hung upon the word; none stirred his head or hand, or looked to right or left, while I declared, in strong terms, 'the grace of our Lord Jesus Christ.'

This sounds an idyllic occasion. Wesley was to visit Widdrington a few more times over the next dozen years but it could never be one of his major centres.

It's interesting that he makes reference to the Jacobite rising of 1715. The more recent events of 1745 were obviously fresh in his mind, and would partly explain this allusion to the earlier rising. But it does seem that Wesley was drawn to the Stuarts, while, of course, renouncing any Jacobite scheme to seize the English crown. A few years later he was standing in Holyrood House, Edinburgh, looking at a portrait of Mary Stuart:[4]

It is scarce possible for any who looks at this to think her such a monster as some have painted her, nor indeed for any who considers the circumstances of her death, equal to that of an ancient martyr.

There's a touch of romantic sentiment here – but also a sense of loyalty to a royal house that in the seventeenth century had to withstand the onslaught of republicans and dissenters. Wesley as a high Tory and an Anglican could not help having sympathy with the Stuart cause. His mother may have been a strong influence here. She regarded King William of Orange, who replaced the Stuart James II in 1688, as a usurper and refused to say Amen at the end of family prayers on his behalf, making her husband so angry that the two parted for some time. Their subsequent reconciliation was the occasion for the conception of their son John, and without that reconciliation there would have been no Methodism! We're digressing – back to Wesley in Northumberland.

From Widdrington Wesley rode the next day to Alnmouth and Alnwick:

Tuesday 19th July (1748): We rode to Alnmouth, a small seaport town, famous for all kinds of wickedness. The people here are sinners convict; they have nothing to pay, but plead guilty before God. Therefore, I preached to them without delay Jesus Christ, for 'wisdom, righteousness, sanctification, and redemption.'

After dinner we rode to Alnwick, one of the largest inland towns in the county of Northumberland. At seven I preached at the cross to as large a congregation as at Newcastle on Sunday evening. This place seemed much to resemble Athlone; all were moved a little, but none very much. The waters spread wide, but not deep; but let the Lord work as it seemeth Him good. [5]

Wesley found Alnmouth a tough nut and had little success here. After a few visits to this 'stupid drowsy people', he gave up trying and abandoned the 'poor, barren place'. Alnwick was a different matter, indeed, after Newcastle it was the place which Wesley was to visit most frequently in the course of his north-eastern work. It had been in important walled town in the Middle ages but by the middle of the eighteenth century the old walls and gates had fallen into disuse and the great castle of the Percys had become ruinous. But Alnwick was enjoying a new prosperity, stimulated by local improvements in farming, trade and the economy generally. The castle was soon to be rebuilt by Hugh, the first duke of Northumberland, and the town was getting some modern buildings, such as the Town Hall and court-house, which on several later visits Wesley was able to use as a preaching room.

The Wesleyan chapel (right) built at Alnwick in 1786, with manse (centre). Both buildings still stand, though have been altered. The chapel is still in use for worship.

The day following his visit to Alnwick Wesley set off northwards to Berwick. He was, of course, travelling up the Great North Road which had been turnpiked only two years before, and much improved, with the expenses recouped by the setting up of tollgates along the route. The mid-eighteenth century saw a vast improvement in the roads of Northumberland, which in most cases were being properly constructed for the first time since the days of the Romans. Even with these improvements the surfaces left much to be desired; but at least travel was safer and easier and this seems to be one of the explanations for Wesley's journeys into Northumberland from 1748 onwards. Let us hear of his first visit to Berwick:[6]

Wednesday 20th July (1748): We took horse between eight and nine, and a little before two came to Berwick. I sent to the commander of the garrison to desire the use of a green place near his house, which he readily granted. I preached at seven to (it was judged) two thousand people. I found the generality of them just as I expected: serious and decent, but not easy to be convinced of anything. For who can tell them what they did not know before?

Thursday, 21st: After preaching we walked round the walls, which they were repairing and rebuilding. I could not but observe to-day how different the face of things was from what it appeared yesterday, especially after I had preached at noon. Yesterday we were hallooed all along the streets; to-day none opened his mouth as we went along – the very children were all silent. The grown people pulled off their hats on every side, so that we might even have fancied ourselves at Newcastle. Oh, well is it that honour is balanced with dishonour, and good report with evil report!

At seven I preached to a far larger congregation than before. And now the word of God was as a fire and an hammer. I began again and again, after I thought I had done; and the latter words were still stronger than the former; so that I was not surprised at the number which attended in the morning, when we had another joyful, solemn hour. Here was the loud call to the people of Berwick, if haply they would know the day of their visitation.

This was an impressive start to Wesley's work in Berwick. We might wish Wesley had spent a little more time to describe the town itself, apart from his brief allusions to the walls and barracks. His first sight of the town as he approached it from the south, and crossed the great seventeenth century bridge over the Tweed with its 15 arches, must surely have excited his imagination yet he doesn't mention it. Berwick was a proud, independent and busy community, and, in those often troubled years, an important military base, the barracks which were built in 1719 said to be the earliest in Britain, and housing about 600 troops. Like most north-eastern towns Berwick got a handsome Town Hall in the eighteenth century, built on Marygate a few years after Wesley's first visit, and as at Alnwick it was to provide him with a place to preach in on his later frequent visits. There was an interesting parish church – one of the very few built under Cromwell – and a number of dissenting congregations, mainly Presbyterian.

On later visits to Berwick Wesley was generally *en route* to or from Scotland, but on this first visit it was the limit of his travels and he turned south to return to Newcastle, preaching at Tughall, Alnwick and Longhorsley on the way. At this latter spot the comment to Wesley of the Church of England parson was very illuminating:[7]

> *Saturday 23rd July 1748: I preached at noon at Long Horsley. The minister here was of a truly moderate spirit. He said, 'I have done all I can for this people; and I can do them no good. Now let others try. If they can do any, I will thank them with all my heart.'*

There is something rather sad about this though one suspects it represents the feelings of a good many parsons who had struggled as best they could to fulfil their office but with little obvious reward. In fact, this was to be Wesley's only visit to Longhorsley so we do not hear from him of any direct result of his work there. He rode back to Newcastle, his head deep in Homer's Iliad.

Between 1748 and 1790 John Wesley was to be up and down the Newcastle to Berwick turnpike some 20 times, mainly on horseback, but in his later years by chaise. These travels constituted one half of his Northumbrian mission – the major half in terms of visits if we leave Newcastle out of his reckoning. The other half was along the Tyne valley, from North Shields and the colliery communities to Hexham and the dales. Vast areas of central and northern

Northumberland were never visited by Wesley at all, and even some important centres such as Wooler, Rothbury and Warkworth received only fleeting visits which were never followed up. This may have been in part due to the remoteness and inaccessibility of some of those areas. When Wesley did make a diversion from the Great North Road to visit other parts it was usually because a road had recently been opened which allowed him to do so. His visit to Rothbury from Alnwick in 1782, for instance, must have been along the so-called Corn Road, which ran from Hexham via Rothbury to Alnmouth, a turnpike constructed in 1751 to expedite the transport of corn for export from Alnmouth. Another new road which Wesley was able to make use of was Field Marshal Wade's 'military road', running along the line of the Roman Wall from Newcastle to Carlisle, and built after the 1745 Jacobite Rising.

There were, however, other reasons why Wesley did not attempt a thorough coverage of Northumberland. Presbyterianism was very strong in the county, especially in the centre and north, where it was virtually an alternative establishment alongside the Church of England. The Presbyterians were not violently against Methodism, but they disliked some of its features and were often impervious to its message. Moreover the character of the people – dour, respectable, fixed in their opinions – also proved a problem. Wesley found it hard to move them, or (as he said of the folk at Berwick) to tell them anything they didn't know already! So although he worked hard in a few key centres, and had some successes, he seems, by and large, to have left the Northumbrians to their Presbyterianism, and Methodism was never to be a strong force in the county, at least north of the coal-bearing zone and the Tyne valley.

Nevertheless, the story of his visits to Northumberland is a very interesting one and becomes more so the more we learn about the social life of the country in Wesley's day, and reconstruct in imagination the places Wesley visited and the routes he travelled. There is, unfortunately, no time to pursue this theme in length here, but a few examples might be mentioned. Let's hear first of another visit to Berwick in September 1749:[8]

> *Sunday, 10th: I preached at eight, and at four in the afternoon, and in the hours between spoke with the members of the society. I met them all at seven, and a glorious meeting it was. I forgot all my pain while we were praising God together; but after they were gone I yielded to*

my friends, and determined to give myself a day's rest. So I spent Monday the 11th in writing; only I could not refrain from meeting the society in the evening. The next evening God enabled me to speak searching words to an earnestly attentive congregation.

That passage gives a nice vignette of Wesley at work, and (more unusually) of Wesley resting. But even in rest he had to be doing something, so he wrote. In fact his beloved Grace Murray was with him in Berwick as he had taken her to work with him among the northern societies, despite the offence and jealousy this caused among the Methodist sisters in Newcastle. At Berwick he fell in love with her more than ever and wrote her life story up to that time – this was the piece of writing he refers to in the passage just quoted. It is sad to recall that within a matter of a couple of weeks or so Grace was to be lost to him for ever. One wonders, incidentally, what the sober citizens of Berwick thought of a woman engaging in active evangelical work, and travelling about the countryside in company with a clerical bachelor.

Many other scenes spring to mind – of Wesley preaching on a windy bowling green at Berwick, in a stuffy crowded Town Hall at Alnwick, in an open site at Saugh House near Cambo where a stone marks the spot and where Methodists gather still today to remember Wesley's work, or standing on a chair to preach in the churchyard at Kelso when Walter Scott, then a boy, was in the congregation and long remembered some of the anecdotes Wesley used.[9] We think too of him preaching at places crowded with soldiers, or panic-stricken at the fears of attack from Spanish and French fleets – all reflecting events in the military history of the reign of George III. We imagine him wandering round the ruins of Warkworth Castle, admiring the newly restored castle at Alnwick and Capability Brown's gardens there, and being shocked at the pictures he saw hanging at Seaton Delaval Hall. We think also of Wesley, with Christopher Hopper, crossing the border into Scotland for the first time (this was in 1751), the two men having to grope their way literally through a Scotch mist!

Saugh House Stone

Let us take leave of Wesley as he describes his visit to Holy Island in 1764:[10]

Wednesday, 23rd May: I rode over the sands to Holy Island, once the famous seat of a bishop; now the residence of a few poor families, who live chiefly by fishing. At one side of the town are the ruins of a cathedral, with an adjoining monastery. It appears to have been a lofty and elegant building, the middle aisle being almost entire. I preached in what was once the market-place to almost all the inhabitants of the island, and distributed some little books among them, for which they were exceeding thankful.

Wesley makes no specific reference to Saint Cuthbert; but he may well have considered (if he knew Bede's life of the saint) how Cuthbert's preaching travels in Northumbria over a thousand years earlier had in many ways been similar in purpose and method to his own – taking the Christian gospel to ordinary folk and winning their response through a combination of powerful gospel preaching and sheer human goodness.

REFERENCES

1. *Eneas Mackenzie, A Historical, Topographical and Descriptive View of the County of Northumberland,* 2 vols. (1825), vol. ii, 179.

2. *Journal iii, 362.*

3. *Ibid., 362.*

4. *Ibid., iv, 455. "Wesley's mother was a decided partisan of the Stuarts", J. C. Bowmer, The Sacrament of the Lord's Supper in Early Methodism, 1951, p.27.*

5. *Wesley had preached at Athlone (in Ireland) for the first time only a few months earlier, on 1st April 1748. On the Alnwick Chapel see T. J. Howells, The Scarecrow Still Stands Mr. Wesley, (Alnwick Chapel, 1786-1986) 1986.*

6. *Journal iii, 363.*

7. *Journal iii, 364.*

8. *Journal iii, 428.*

9. *The stone at Saugh House has the following inscription:*

   John Wesley preached here
   on his 79th birthday
   June 17th 1782.

   Oddly enough, though Wesley was certainly born on 17th June 1703, he was by 1782 celebrating 28th June as the date of his birthday, as an entry to his journal for that year makes clear. The reason was that in 1752 England accepted the continental Gregorian calendar, one consequence being the removal of 11 days from that year, between 2nd and 14th September. Wesley accepted the logic of this, and from 1752 moved his birthday on from 17th June to 28th June, counting the 17th as one of the 11 days removed.

10. *Journal v, 70.*

The Octagon Chapel – Yarm on Tees, 1763-64.
Still used for worship.

IX

JOHN WESLEY IN THE DALES

Even the most casual traveller through the Pennine dales can hardly fail to notice the Methodist chapels. There they stand, grey and respectable, solidly built in local stone, sometimes large and ambitious, more often modest and unadorned except for a carefully carved date stone, and often standing in their own burial grounds. You'll see them in pretty well every township and village, and even in small and remote hamlets in the upper parts of the valleys. The churches of other denominations are, of course, there as well, but nowhere near as numerous. During the past 20 years a number of these chapels have closed as young people have had to move away to find work. But, in some cases, the congregations that gather are worshipping in buildings which John Wesley himself knew and preached in, places sanctified by over two centuries of Christian prayer and praise in the Methodist tradition. How did it all begin? And why did the dales prove such hospitable ground in which Methodism might grow?

What is certainly true is that it was not all due to John Wesley. If you add up the number of days spent by Wesley in Wensleydale, Swaledale, Teesdale, Weardale, Allendale and Derwentdale over a period of nearly 50 years the total comes to little more than two months altogether! There could hardly be a clearer demonstration of the fact that Methodism was not the product of one man's labours, even though we must obviously take account of the powerful if indirect influence exercised by Wesley in his absence through his writings, his inspired organisation, and the preachers whom he appointed to work under his direction. We'll come back a little later to consider the work of Wesley and these other preachers, but we must also look at other general influences which favoured Methodism in the dales.

They were remote places in Wesley's day, tough environments in which generations of hill farmers had tried to wrest a living. But though remote they were not undeveloped. Indeed, in the eighteenth century they were filled with all the sights, sounds and smells of lead mining and lead smelting. The dales were far more populous and prosperous than now. And lead mining, just like hill farming, did much to fashion the character of the people engaged in it. Let's hear that old historian Eneas Mackenzie, as he describes this particular group of men. He is writing a few decades after Wesley but his account holds good for the earlier years:[1]

High House, Weardale, 1760-61, still in use
(Enlarged in the later 19th century)

Newbiggin in Teesdale, 1759-60. Still used on special occasions.

There are some circumstances in the character of the lead-miners which distinguish them from every other class of workmen. These peculiarities necessarily arise from the nature of their employment, which is extremely hazardous and uncertain. The expense of sinking the shafts, and cutting adits, lies with the adventurer, who furnishes also the machinery for the works. The miners then agree to drive the vein and raise the ore (finding their own tools, candles, gunpowder, etc.), on the condition of their receiving a certain proportion of the profits of the ore produced, be it little or much.

The circumstances of this uncertainty of their gains has a marked effect upon their character. The activity which hope inspires keeps their minds lively and acute, and prevents that dullness which generally characterises other labourers.

The miners are as much distinguished for an unbending spirit of independence as for intellectual activity and acquirements. They work in partnership of four, six or eight, and divide their wages equally amongst them. Uncontrolled by the mandates of a master or overseer, they rely solely upon their own judgement and experience, and often lighten their labour by amusing or instructive conversation. Nor is it uncommon to hear them dispute on metaphysical and philological subjects, or on the various doctrines of political economy.

Folk like this were well able to judge for themselves the virtues or otherwise of Methodism, and they possessed the independence to decide freely for themselves whether or not they would give it their loyalty. Once given, their loyalty was firm, intelligent and strong; and the chapels, built out of their own pockets and often partly by their own labours, soon became focal points of communal life, centres not only for worship but also for education, fellowship and social activities of many kinds. This does not mean that all lead miners and their families became Methodists; nor does it mean that Methodism was free from opposition and persecution in the dales. Nevertheless there was a strong basic inclination in favour of Methodism.

The religious history of the dales was also an important factor. The Church of England had never really won the hearts and minds of the dalesfolk – the parishes, such as Stanhope in Weardale with its 50,000 acres, were too vast and remote for the clergy to exercise any strong pastoral oversight. In consequence nonconformity had taken root. Congregationalists, Baptists, Presbyterians and Quakers were all active and you can still find a sprinkling of old Quaker meeting houses and other old Dissenting chapels around the dales.[2] Methodism was able to build upon these older Dissenting traditions and in some cases to attract members from them, because of its novelty, liveliness and enthusiasm.

It is time we turned from generalities to specific places and people, and first to Wesley in particular. In the autumn of 1743 he paid a brief visit to Wensleydale and preached there in Wensley Church, and was back the following year preaching also at Redmire and Castle Bolton. But his first visit to the lead mining dales further north did not take place until the spring of 1747:[3]

> *Tuesday, 24th March: I rode to Blanchland, about twenty miles from Newcastle. The rough mountains round about were still white with snow. In the midst of them is a small winding valley, through which the Derwent runs. On the edge of this the little town stands, which is indeed little more than a heap of ruins. There seems to have been a large cathedral church, by the vast walls which still remain. I stood in the churchyard, under one side of the building, upon a large tombstone, round which, while I was at prayers, all the congregation kneeled down on the grass. They were gathered out of the lead-mines from all parts; many from Allendale, six miles off. A row of little children sat under the opposite wall, all quiet and still. The whole congregation drank in every word, with such earnestness in their looks, I could not but hope that God will make this wilderness sing for joy.*

There is something strangely evocative about this account. The whole scene comes alive in the imagination – the quiet, cold day, the lonely narrow valley, the rushing waters of the Derwent, the tumbledown village not yet restored by the Crewe trustees who acquired it a few years later, and the gaunt remains of the medieval abbey under whose wall Wesley stood and preached to the earnest, silent congregation. It is one of those occasions in Wesley's life at which one would particularly like to have been present. Standing in Blanchland churchyard today it is still possible to recreate the scene, though there is no tombstone now surviving which is old enough to have been that on which Wesley stood to preach. He was obviously expected on this first visit, the folk having gathered specially to hear him; news of Wesley's work in the colliery areas and the Tyne valley had obviously reached these lonely parts.

Some 15 months later he was back at Blanchland again and was recommended by the steward of the mines to ride on to Baybridge where the miners were all gathered for the bi-annual pay day, providing Wesley with a large ready-made congregation. A couple of days later he was in Allendale town for a similar occasion, and in between had also paid visits to Nenthead and Alston, staying overnight at Hindley Hill farm in the lower part of Allendale, near the junction of the East and West Allen rivers. Hindley Hill was a farmstead of the Broadwood family, and had become the base for Christopher Hopper, the Ryton preacher who has appeared several times in these chapters. He worked the area in a permanent way which Wesley was not able to do, and established a good many Methodist Societies, one of which, built between 1751 and 1752 at Keenley, near Hindley Hill, was the second purpose-built Methodist chapel in the north-east, the Orphan House at Newcastle having been the first a decade earlier.[4] Hopper once explained to another preacher his mode of work in those early years:[5]

> *Our plan was to visit a town or village, and ask permission to expound the word of God in one of their houses or cottages; if the people did not invite us to lodge and break bread with them, after repeating our visit two or three times, we took it as an indication that we were not called to such a place.*

He then described a visit made by himseif and Alexander Mather, a Scottish preacher from Brechin, to the Alston area. They tried one place and found no hospitality at all, so gave it up.[6]

> *Proceeding to the next village, an old woman came out from a small cottage, and stretching forth her withered arms, blessed us in the name of the Lord Jesus, invited us into her humble dwelling, and spreading before us her whole stock of provision, which consisted of three apples and five potatoes, she bade us welcome, saying that had*

she possessed more, we, as the ambassadors of Christ, should have been welcome to it. I looked at Mr. Mather, and told him it was a token we were called to that place, eating and drinking according to the Apostolic plan, when we were asked; there we preached and there a society was established.

Late in 1748 Hopper, with some Methodists from Allendale, made an exploratory venture into Weardale. Let us hear his own account:[7]

It was in a storm of snow that we crossed the quagmires and enormous mountains. When we came into the dales, we met with a very cold reception. The enemy had barricaded the place, and made his bulwarks strong. But the Lord made way for His truth. He opened the heart of a poor Scotch shepherd to receive us into his little thatched cabin, where we lodged all night.

The next day I preached under the walls of an old castle. A few children and two or three old women attended, who looked hard at us. When I had done we followed them into their houses, and talked freely to them in their own language about the kingdom of God. They heard, and obeyed the Gospel. The next evening I had a large congregation, who heard with much attention, and received the word gladly. Some time after I preached in private houses, ale-houses, cockpits, or wherever I could find a door open. The fire then spread from heart to heart, and God was glorified.

This was the beginning of a good work in Weardale, which has continued and increased to this day.

The castle Hopper refers to was at Westgate, but does not survive today. The work he began in Weardale was taken up by other preachers, notably by Jacob Rowell, a native of Whitfield in Allendale, who while on his way to a cock fight had been converted by a sermon preached by Hopper in Allendale town in 1748. Under Rowell and other preachers Methodism in Weardale gathered strength. Meanwhile the work had begun in Teesdale, both at Barnard Castle under a shoemaker called Joseph Cheeseborough, and in the upper parts of the dale around Newbiggin under Jacob Rowell and others. It was from Newbiggin that two brothers took

Methodism to the little hamlet of Blades near Low Row in Swaledale, where William Spensley fitted up a cottage near his home for worship – the first Methodist preaching room in the dale. This was very much the pattern of things in early Methodism, with the work spreading from dale to dale as the result of the witness of plain folk, whose words and example sparked a response in others of like mind.

John Wesley does not enter the scene again until 1752 when he spent a couple of days in Teesdale, Weardale and Allendale, the fire engine being hauled out at Barnard Castle in an attempt to scatter his congregation. It was another nine years before he was back in the dales, by which time an enormous Dales Circuit had been established with its base in Barnard Castle, and covering all the territory between Tynedale and Wensleydale (from north to south) and between Darlington and Penrith (east to west). Jacob Rowell was the first of Wesley's preachers to be put in charge of this Circuit which by 1772 had 27 scattered Societies with a thousand members. The strongest centres were upper Weardale, Teesdale, and the Low Row area of Swaledale. The Dales Circuit was founded in 1757 and on 11th January the following year Jacob Rowell presented himself at the Quarter Sessions in Durham City to receive his formal certificate as a licensed preacher. This involved affirming his loyalty to the Protestant house of Hanover, his opposition to the Jacobites and the Papists, and his acceptance of most of the Thirty-nine Articles of the *Book of Common Prayer*. By such a process nonconformist ministers and preachers were legally enabled to carry on their work under the Toleration Act of 1689.[8]

Barnard Castle 173.
Catherston — 13
Lune — — 12
Teasdale — 63
Richmond — 16.
Hudswell — 10
Wensidale — 8.
Swaledale — 84
Keath — 23
Yorkendale — 38.
Barningim — 19.
Stainmoore — 15.
Soulby — 19.
Longemartin 7
Westmerby — 31
Alston — 39.
West Allon — 25.
East Allon — 46
Hole house — 16.
Hexhamshire 20
Sedham — 14
Weardale — 266.
Wolvingim 40
Breckonhil 19.
Grainge — 15
West Hucklon 8.
Elastlim — 4
In all — 1003 In the year 1772

*Methodist membership in the Dales Circuit 1772, from the pocket books
of Jacob Rowell who served in this Circuit for several years
(Reproduced with permission Durham County Record Office)*

Under the guidance of full-time preachers like Jacob Rowell, assisted by a growing number of laymen and women, Methodism took firm root in the dale. From 1761 Wesley began a regular series of pastoral and preaching tours of the dales, returning there virtually every two years up to his last visit in 1790. Time forbids any detailed account of these tours, but let's get the flavour of them by dipping into Wesley's journal for 1768:[9]

Wednesday, June 1st: I preached in Teesdale. The sun was scorching hot when I began, but was soon covered with clouds. Many of the militia were present at Barnard Castle in the evening, and behaved with decency.

Thursday, 2nd: I preached, at noon, at a farmer's house, near Brough, in Westmorland. The sun was hot enough, but some shady trees covered both me and most of the congregation. A little bird perched on one of them, and sung without intermission, from the beginning of the service unto the end.

The evening congregation in Swaledale was far larger, and equally attentive; and the society was one of the most lively which I have met with in England. Many of them do rejoice in the pure love of God, and many more are earnestly seeking it.

Friday, 3rd: I rode to Richmond, intending to preach near the house of one of our friends; but some of the chief of the town sent to desire me to preach in the market-place. The Yorkshire militia were all there, just returned from their exercise; and a more rude rabble-rout I never saw; without sense, decency, or good manners.

In the evening (at Barnard Castle) the commanding officer gave orders there should be no exercise, that all the Durham militia (what a contrast!) might be at liberty to attend the preaching. Accordingly, we had a little army of officers as well as soldiers; and all behaved well. A large number of them were present at five in the morning. I have not found so deep and lively a work in any part of the kingdom as runs through the whole circuit, particularly in the vales that wind between these horrid mountains. I returned to Newcastle in the evening.

By this time more chapels had been built and it is good to know the chapel at Ireshopeburn in Weardale is still open for worship and to visit today. Newbiggin in Teesdale chapel is open for special services, and can be visited by arrangement.   The chapel at Ireshopeburn, called High House, experienced a very remarkable revival in 1772 which Wesley described meticulously in his journal.

The mountains may have seemed horrid to Wesley as he toiled over their uncertain roads in all weathers, but the dales and their people he undoubtedly loved.   Apart from their religious zeal, their hospitality was warm and generous. Of the Society at Weardale he wrote:[10]

> They have been the most liberal in providing everything needful for the preachers.

As we leave the dales let us allow Christopher Hopper the last words, by quoting a verse composed by him as he rode from Cumbria into Weardale and contemplated the restoration of the inner man that he could expect there:[11]

> The promised land from Kilhope top
> I now exult to see.
> My hope is full (O glorious hope!)
> Of good spice cake and tea!

REFERENCES

1. Mackenzie *op. cit.*, i, 206-7.

2. For example, Quaker Meeting houses at Bainbridge, Countersett, Allendale Town and Alston; Baptist chapels at Hamsterley and Wolsingham; Independent (Congregational) chapels at Low Row (Swaledale), Keld, Garrigill, Alston, *et. al.*

3. *Journal*, iii, 286.

4. The chapel at Keenley is still standing (in its own burial ground) though has been altered since Wesley's day.

5. *Steele*, p.105.

6. *Ibid.*, pp.105-6.

7. *E.M.P.*, i, 198-99.

8. Rowell's pocket-books are in the County Durham Record Office, as is the preacher's licence mentioned here.

9. *Journal*, v, 275-76.

10. *Journal.*, v, 466.

11. *Methodist Recorder Winter Number*, 1898, p.33.

X

THE END OF THE JOURNEY

By my reckoning John Wesley visited the north-east of England on 48 occasions – this is counting all his separate arrivals from either the south or from Scotland. These visits were spread over a period of almost exactly 48 years, from the first arrival in May 1742 to the last in June 1790. When he first came he was 38, and when his visits finally ended he was almost 87.   This is all remarkable enough. But what we must also remember is that this was only one part of Wesley's total mission.   In the course of his north-eastern tours he was always coming from and going to other areas, in which he repeated the evangelistic and pastoral work which he did here. In order to get a true estimate of Wesley's total work we have, therefore, to multiply his north-eastern mission a good many times over, and imagine similar endeavours in Scotland, in Cumbria, in Yorkshire, in the Midlands, in the south-west, in Wales, in Ireland, in the eastern counties, in London, and so on. It all adds up to one of the most sustained and impressive missionary undertakings in the whole of Christian history.

Why did he do it?   By now I think the answer will be clear.   He regarded this work as his special vocation, a calling from God which once taken up he found impossible to relinquish.   Let us remind ourselves of his great aim, in his own words:[1]

> To promote, as far as I am able, vital, practical religion, and by the grace of God to beget, preserve, and increase the life of God in the souls of men.

Of course, once the work had begun it acquired a momentum of its own. Wesley saw it initially as reviving the Church of England, and religion generally, not creating a new Church or sect.   But nevertheless as Methodism grew it developed its own character and life.   How did Wesley see the character and purpose of the Methodists?[2]

> We look upon the Methodists (so called) in general, not as any particular party (this would exceedingly obstruct the

grand design for which we conceive God has raised them up) but as living witnesses, in and to every party of that Christianity which we preach, which is hereby demonstrated to be a real thing and visibly held out to all the world . . . By Methodists I mean a people who prefer to pursue holiness of heart and life, inward and outward conformity in all things to the revealed will of God; more particularly in justice, mercy, and truth or universal love filling the heart and governing the life.

In the execution of this great enterprise Wesley was obviously sustained and strengthened by his profound faith in the power of God working in and through him. His exclamation was not 'Look what I have done', but rather 'What hath God wrought!'* Nevertheless, the personality, the courage, and the sheer stamina of the man himself all played their part. Wesley himself, as he grew older, usually around the time of his birthday, was wont to think about his health, and his ability to keep going at an age when other men would have long since sought a well-deserved retirement. On Monday 27th June 1774 he left Newcastle and rode to Stockton, stayed overnight there and then wrote this entry in his journal:[3]

Tuesday 28th June: This being my birthday, the first day of my seventy-second year, I was considering, how is this, that I find just the same strength as I did thirty years ago? That my sight is considerably better now, and my nerves firmer than they were then? That I have none of the infirmities of old age, and have lost several that I had in my youth?

The grand cause is the good pleasure of God, who doeth whatsoever pleaseth Him. The chief means are

(1) my constantly rising at four for about fifty years;

(2) my generally preaching at five in the morning – one of the most healthy exercises in the world;

(3) my never travelling less, by sea or land, than four thousand five hundred miles in a year.

---

*See, for instance, *Journal*, vi, 18, 103, 246. viii, 38.

How about that as a personal recipe for health and fitness! There's little doubt that Wesley's constant exercise, his careful diet, his complete lack of self-indulgence, all kept his slight frame tough and lean. He actually welcomed challenges to bodily discipline. In warm weather he loved to sleep outside on the ground, and did this for forty years until the age of 72, when the practice led to a serious illness and had to be abandoned.[4] On the eve of his 77th birthday he climbed the tower of Boston parish church in Lincolnshire, the famous 'Boston Stump', which meant an ascent of 364 steps to a height of 282 feet – and he was still able to enjoy the view from the top! One secret of Wesley's energy was a knack he shared with other great men, the ability to 'cat nap' at any time.

Here is how an old Victorian minister John Ward, described this in his account of Methodism in Swaledale:[5]

> *Mr Wesley always made his home at the house of the Spensleys up at Blades. A few traditionary circumstances in connection with his visits are still remembered. It Is well known that such was the complete mastery which he had gained over himself that he could command sleep at any moment he desired. He has been known to catch a few moments slumber in the pulpit during the interval of singing a hymn. It is said that on one occasion he arrived at Low Row an hour before the time of service, and being weary with his journey, he requested the old lady of the house to procure him a pillow and a sheet; with these he threw himself upon a table, telling her that she might go about her usual work as it would not disturb him and he would take care to wake up at the proper time. Upon this hard bed he slept soundly for an hour, and woke up to the minute to meet his congregation when it arrived.*

Wesley was able to survive a variety of accidents with little apparent damage. One of these happened when he was almost 79, and about to go from Kelso to Alnwick:[6]

> *Saturday 15th June (1782): As I was coming downstairs, the carpet slipped from under my feet, which, I know not how, turned me round, and pitched me back, with my head foremost, for six or seven stairs. It was impossible to recover myself till I came to the bottom. My head rebounded once or twice from the edge of the stone stairs.*

But it felt to me exactly as if I had fallen on a cushion or a pillow. Dr. Douglas ran out, sufficiently affrighted. But he needed not. For I rose as well as ever; having received no damage, but the loss of a little skin from one or two of my fingers. Doth God give His angels charge over us, to keep us in all our ways?

In the evening, and on Sunday the 16th preached at Alnwick.

A more dangerous threat to his life had in fact occurred in 1774, just a few days before the entry quoted earlier in which he analysed his own health and strength. The incident is vivid, and worth hearing in some detail. It also introduces us to William Smith, a prosperous Newcastle corn merchant and a leading Methodist in the city, who married Jane Vazeille, the daughter of Wesley's wife by her first husband. William Smith, therefore, was Wesley's stepson-in-law, and his little daughters, Mary and Jane, were regarded by Wesley as his grandchildren, and they, as we shall hear, were accustomed to calling him 'Grandpapa', which I find rather appealing, and which I'm sure must have delighted Wesley, and warmed the old man's heart. Here is Wesley's account of the incident:[7]

Monday 20th June (1774): About nine I set out from Newcastle for Horsley, with Mr. Hopper and Mr. Smith. I took Mrs. Smith and her two little girls in the chaise with me. About two miles from the town, just on the brow of the hill, on a sudden both the horses set out, without any visible cause, and flew down the hill like an arrow out of a bow. In a minute John fell off the coach-box. The horses then went on full-speed, sometimes to the edge of the ditch on the right, sometimes on the left. A cart came up against them; they avoided it as exactly as if a man had been on the box. A narrow bridge was at the foot of the hill; they went directly over the middle of it. They ran up the next hill with the same speed, many persons meeting us, but getting out of the way. Near the top of the hill was a gate, which led into a farmer's yard. It stood open. They turned short and ran through it, without touching the gate on one side or the post on the other. I thought, 'However, the gate which is on the other side of the yard, and is shut, will stop them.' But they rushed through it as if it had been held a cobweb, and galloped on through the cornfield. The little girls cried out,

87

'Grandpapa, save us!' I told them, 'Nothing will hurt you; do not be afraid'; feeling no more fear or care (blessed be God!) than if I had been sitting in my study.

The horses ran on until they came to the edge of a steep precipice. Just then Mr. Smith, who could not overtake us before, galloped in between. They stopped in a moment. Had they gone on ever so little, he and we must have gone down together!

I am persuaded both evil and good angels had a large share in this transaction; how large we do not know now, but we shall know hereafter.

Being the sort of man he was, Wesley went on to make a cool analysis in his journal of the whole incident, and recognised in it a whole chain of providential circumstances. It was indeed a dangerous incident and might have shortened his life by 17 years.

Wesley tells us here that he was in a chaise. This became his usual mode of transport in his later years, allowing him greater comfort and relaxation, the opportunity for an occasional nap, and greater ease in reading books which he loved to do while travelling. However, even at an advanced age, he occasionally was prepared to abandon the chaise and get on to a horse, when the terrain demanded it. One such occasion was in 1780 (he was 76 at the time) and he had to get from Wensleydale to Swaledale:[8]

Wednesday 3rd May: Judging it impracticable to pass the mountains in a carriage, I sent my chaise round and took horse. At twelve I preached at Swaledale to a loving people, increasing both in grace and number. Thence we crossed over another range of dreary mountains, and in the evening reached Barnard Castle. Not being yet inured to riding, I now felt something like weariness. But I forgot it in the lively congregation, and in the morning it was gone.

Thursday 4th: About eight I preached to a serious congregation at Cotherstone, and about one at Newbiggin in Teesdale. We doubted how we should get over the next mountain, the famous Pikelaw, after so long and heavy rains; but I scarce ever remember us getting over it so well. We found the people in Weardale, as usual, some of the liveliest in the kingdom, knowing nothing, and desiring to know nothing, save Jesus Christ and Him crucified.

THE SABBATH-DAYS PLAN

FOR THE

Traveling and Local Preachers in Barnard-Caſtle Circuit.

"Rather break a Leg than miſs your Appointment."—Mr WESLEY.

"Our Sufficiency is of GOD."—St PAUL.

Preachers.

1. C. Winfield.
2. J. Forſter.
3. L. Barlow.
4. S. Uſtroyd.
5. J. Wilkin.
6. W. Diſonl.
7. H. Oliver.
8. R. Clarkſon.
9. G. Powell.
10. T. Blackburn.
11. A. Race.
12. J. Myers.
13. J. Phillipſon.
14. J. Featherſton.
15. J. Dacelym.
16. J. Parker.
17. J. Vickers.
18. J. Vipond.
19. J. Thompſon.
20. J. Forſter.

Places: Barnard-Caſtle, Bowes, Newſham, Scargill, Mickleton and Eggleſton, Cotherſton, Staindrop, Evenwood, Biſhop—Auckland, Newbiggin and Middleton, High-beaſe, Wolgate, Ditto, Eaſtgate, Rookhope, Stanhope, Froſterly, Wolſingham, Thornley, Creek.

Months: November 1807, December, January 1808, February, March, April.

Printed by Edward Walker, Newcaſtle.

N. B. January 5th Quarter-Day at Barnard-Caſtle, and April 3d at High-Houſe, and a Love Feaſt.

An early preaching plan for the Barnard Castle Circuit, 1807-8, part of the much larger Dales Circuit which had been formed in 1757. The first three names in the preachers' list are the full-time ministers, the rest are laymen (i.e. local preachers).[9] (Reproduced with permission Durham County Record Office)

Four years later, aged 80, the veteran traveller did much the same again:[10]

> *Thursday 10th June (1784): After preaching at five, I took horse for the Dales, and about eight preached at Cotherstone. Here I had the pleasure of seeing some of our brethren who had been long at variance cordially reconciled. Hence we rode through rain and wind to Newbiggin-in-Teesdale. Being but a poor horseman, and having a rough horse, I had just strength for my journey and none to spare; but, after resting a while I preached without any weariness.*
>
> *Having then procured an easier horse, I rode over the great mountain into Weardale.*

Wesley's final visits to our area were in 1790. He came north in early May, travelled via Newcastle into Scotland, but very soon returned from the north via Carlisle to pay his last farewell to his beloved Methodist Societies in the north-east. On his arrival at Darlington from the south he had been met by William Smith, his stepson-in-law, and Charles Atmore, one of the Methodist preachers. Atmore described him thus:[11]

> *We heard him preach. He appears very feeble; and no wonder . . . His sight has failed so much that he cannot see to give out the hymn; yet his voice is strong, and his spirits remarkably lively. Surely this great and good man is the prodigy of the age.*

We perhaps can best get the flavour of this last tour, which had about it something of the air of a poignant yet triumphal farewell procession, by letting Wesley's journal entries speak for themselves. We hear first not from his full journal, but from his supplementary diary which summarised in rather staccato form the doings of each day which, as we shall see, began at crack of dawn with a cup of tea. We find him at Darlington:[12]

> *Thursday 6th May (1790): 3.30 Tea; 4 chaise; 7 Durham, tea; 8 chaise; 10.30 Newcastle, on business; 1 at brother Smith's, dinner, conversed, visited, sleep; 4 prayed; 4.30 Isaiah lvii, 1,2; 7.30 the bands, supper, conversed, prayer; 9.30.*

Friday 7th: 4.30 Prayed, letters; 6 within to many; 8 tea, conversed, prayer; 9 letters; 1 within to many; 2 dinner, visited, sleep; 4.15 prayed, tea, conversed; 6.30 Psalm xxxiv. 11! select society; 8 supper, conversed, prayer; 9.30.

The texts quoted are those on which Wesley either meditated, or used in his preaching to the various groups he met (the bands, the select society and so on), and each day ended with him retiring at 9.30 prompt.

About a month later he was back in Newcastle after his visit to Scotland:[13]

Friday 4th June: (1790) We reached Newcastle. In this and Kingswood house, were I to do my own will, I should choose to spend the short remainder of my days. But it cannot be; this is not my rest. This and the next evening we had a numerous congregation, and the people seemed much alive.

Sunday 6th: I was invited to preach in Lamesley church, on the side of Gateshead Fell; but, some hours after, the minister changed his mind. So I preached in our own preaching-house, which contained the greater part of the congregation tolerably well; among whom were Sir Henry Liddell and his Lady, with a great number of his servants.

The chapel was hot as a stove, but neither high nor low seemed to regard it; for God was there. The Orphan House was equally crowded in the evening; but the rain would not suffer me to preach abroad.

Monday 7th: I transcribed the stations of the preachers.

Tuesday 8th: I wrote a form for settling the preaching-houses, without any superfluous words, which shall be used for the time to come, verbatim, for all the houses to which I contribute anything. I will no more encourage that villainous tautology of lawyers, which is the scandal of our nation. In the evening I preached to the children of our Sunday school, six or seven hundred of whom were present. N. B. – None of our masters or mistresses teach for pay. They seek a reward that man cannot give.

Wednesday 9th: Having dispatched all the business I had to do here, in the evening I took a solemn leave of this lovely people, perhaps never to see them more in this life, and set out early in the morning.

These entries give various indications of the fruits of Wesley's work in the north-east. Newcastle had meant a great deal to him for many years, ('lovely place, lovely people' he once declared!) – and had become not only a strong and lively Methodist centre but a base from which the work had spread. Having been the centre of one enormous preaching circuit, covering all the north-east, it had seen important daughter circuits gain their own independence as the number of members and preachers increased and as Methodist organisation became stronger in various localities, so that by the end of Wesley's life we find a developing pattern of circuit organisation based on places such as Sunderland, Barnard Castle (for the Dales), Hexham, Yarm and Stockton, Alnwick, Berwick, Dunbar and Edinburgh. In all these places, and in many others, chapels had been built and Methodism was growing in strength, respectability and influence. Just two years before this final visit Wesley had preached near the Keelmen's Hospital and his mind had gone back 46 years to the first sermons he preached in Newcastle, there and on the Quayside, in 1742. What changes he had witnessed since those early days! Many of those changes were, of course, due to his own punctilious care and oversight, still as strong as ever as, during this final visit, he stations the preachers for the last time and clarifies the legal position of the preaching houses.

His thoughts at this time might also have returned to the formerly wild colliers of Chowdene, across the Tyne on Gateshead Fell. The fruits of work among them had also been considerable. In April 1765 Wesley noted in his journal:[14]

The chapel at Keenley in Allendale (built 1751) shown before the alterations of the later nineteenth century. It is still in use, and has a burial ground adjoining.

Thursday 18th April: At 3 I preached to the poor colliers in Gateshead Fell. How do these shame the colliers of Kingswood! flocking from all parts on the weekdays as well as Sundays; such a thirst have they after the good word!

The place they flocked to was the chapel on the Fell of 1754, one of the earliest in the north-east to be built after the Orphan House in Newcastle. Here it was that Wesley preached on that last Sunday on Tyneside in June 1790 after Lamesley Church had been closed to him. The presence of Sir Henry and Lady Liddell from Ravensworth Castle was a clear sign of the regard that Wesley had won, and may have prompted in him a wry inward smile as he compared the respectable assembly before him with those half-naked, starving children who crowded round him on his first visit to Chowdene years before.

And then Wesley mentions the Sunday Schools, which Methodism was doing so much to foster in centres like Newcastle, Sunderland, Stockton and so on, taking up the initiative of Robert Raikes who began Sunday School work in Gloucester about 1780. It could be argued that it was through Sunday Schools that Methodism was to achieve its widest religious, educational and social influence in the age of the Industrial Revolution.

So Wesley bade his farewell to Tyneside; and after visiting Weardale, Durham, Sunderland, Hartlepool, Stockton and Yarm, set off south for the very last time. His travelling days were almost done and he was to die in London on 2nd March following, in 1791, at the age of 87. A fine memorial was erected in Wesley's Chapel on the City Road in London. It describes John Wesley in these words:

A man in learning and sincere piety scarcely inferior to any:
In zeal, ministerial labour and extensive usefulness
Superior perhaps to all men
Since the days of St. Paul.

Regardless of fatigue, personal danger and disgrace
He went out into the highways and hedges
Calling sinners to repentance
And publishing the Gospel of Peace.

In 1875 a memorial in Westminster Abbey was erected to the honour of John and Charles Wesley. On it are to be found three sayings of Wesley himself:

The World is my parish.

The best of all is, God is with us.

God buries his workmen and carries on his work.

Perhaps these simple phrases sum up better than any other the essence of that very remarkable travelling preacher, John Wesley.

Memorial of John and Charles Wesley at Westminster Abbey, dated 1875. The words commemorate John Wesley's final message before he died.

To the memory of
THE VENERABLE JOHN WESLEY A.M.
This GREAT LIGHT arose
(By the singular Providence of GOD)
to enlighten THESE NATIONS
And to revive, enforce and defend
The pure Apostolical DOCTRINES and PRACTICES of
THE PRIMITIVE CHURCH:
Which he continued to do both by his WRITINGS and his LABOURS
For more than HALF A CENTURY:
And, to his inexpressible Joy,
Not only beheld their INFLUENCE extending
And their EFFICACY witness'd
In the Hearts and Lives of MANY THOUSANDS
As well in THE WESTERN WORLD as in THESE KINGDOMS:
But also, far above all human Power of Expectation,
Lived to see PROVISION made by the Singular Grace of God
For their CONTINUANCE and ESTABLISHMENT
TO THE JOY OF FUTURE GENERATIONS
READER, if thou art constrained to bless the INSTRUMENT
GIVE GOD THE GLORY
After having languished a few days, He at length
Fulfilled his COURSE and his LIFE together, GLORIOUSLY
Triumphing over DEATH March 2nd An. Dom. 1791 in the
Eighty Eighth year of his age

The inscription from the memorial marking Wesley's grave
in the burial ground behind Wesley's Chapel, City Road, London.
The memorial was erected by the Wesleyan preachers in 1839
to mark the centenary of the beginning of Methodism.

REFERENCES

1. P. S. Watson, _The Message of the Wesleys_ (1964), p.29.

2. _Ibid._, p.30.

3. _Journal_, vi, 29.

4. J. Wesley, _Sermons on Several Occasions,_ 2 vols., 1834, vol. i. Introduction, p.32.

5. John Ward, _Methodism in Swaledale_, 1865, pp.24-25.

6. _Journal_, vi, 358.

7. _Ibid._, vi, 27. Some information on William Smith's daughters can be found in G. J. Stevenson, _City Road Chapel_, 1872, pp.359-60, 473-75. Jane married Christopher Sundius, a merchant, and one of the 16 founders of the Bible Society in 1804. Mary married a Wesleyan minister, the Revd. John Stamp, whose son was the author of _The Orphan House of Wesley_ published in 1863 – a remarkable compilation of information on the first hundred years of Methodism in and around Newcastle. William Smith's portrait hangs in the vestry of Brunswick Methodist Church, Newcastle, and his gravestone, which gives details of other members of his family also, is in St. Andrew's Churchyard, Newcastle.

8. _Journal_, vi, 276.

9. This is one of the earliest printed plans to survive. The first three in the list of preachers are the ministers (travelling preachers) and the others are lay (local) preachers. Barnard Castle had ministerial appointments every Sunday while some chapels never heard a minister (on Sundays at least) during the entire six months covered by the plan. The hours of service at the chapels allowed Methodists also to attend matins and evensong at their parish churches, a practice which was encouraged by the Wesleyans at that time but not universally popular. The letters which occur against some dates mean as follows: S: Sacrament (Holy Communion). L: Lovefeast. T: Tickets (i.e. the quarterly distribution of membership tickets to the Methodist classes). Ministers officiated at all of these. The 'Quarter Days' mentioned at the foot of the plan were the Circuit Quarterly Meetings. A. Race (among the local preachers) is Anthony Race (1751-1818) a Weardale lead miner converted when a boy by Wesley; he received a licence to preach in 1779. His appointments on this plan are all in Weardale chapels (probably with regard to his age or infirmity) but as recently at 1805 he had walked to appointments in Alston and Nenthead. His son (also Anthony) became a Primitive Methodist preacher, and his grandson (George Race) was

a well known dales character. There is a finely carved gravestone in Barnard Castle churchyard to another of the preachers on the plan, William Dixon, who died in 1820 aged 60.

10. *Journal, vi, 515.*

11. *Journal, viii, 63 note 2.*

12. *Ibid., viii, 64.*

13. *Journal, viii, 69.*

14. *Ibid., v, iii.*

GUIDE TO FURTHER READING

I WESLEY'S OWN WRITINGS

The Journal of the Revd. John Wesley, edited by Nehemiah Curnock, 8 vols., 1909-16. 1938.

The Letters of John Wesley, edited by John Telford, 8 vols., 1931.

(These 'Standard' editions of Wesley's journal and correspondence are currently being replaced by new editions of all Wesley's works. However, it will be a good many years before the new series is complete and the Standard editions remain the accessible source.)

P. S. Watson (ed.), The Message of the Wesleys, 1964 (a valuable compilation of extracts).

Gordon Wakefield (ed.), The Fire of Love: The Spirituality of John Wesley, 1976. (a much briefer set of extracts than Watson's).

There have been various abridged editions of Wesley's Journal, offering a selection of entries from the full account. Most are out of print though are occasionally available second-hand (e.g. by Hugh Martin, S.C.M. Press 1955, or N. Curnock, Epworth Press 1903/1952) but a new abridgement has recently appeared: The Journal of John Wesley, abridged by Christopher Idle, Lion Paperback, 1986. While the older editions are still of value, Idle's can be recommended and has the advantage of being available in bookshops.

II HISTORIES OF METHODISM

W. J. Townsend, H. B. Workman, and G. Eayrs (ed.), A New History of Methodism, 2 vols., 1909, (no longer 'new' but still of value).

R. Davies, A. Raymond George, and G. Rupp (eds.), <u>A History of the Methodist Church in Great Britain</u>, vol. (i) 1965, vol. (ii) 1978, vol. (iii) 1983, vol. (iv) 1988.

(The standard modern history, vol.(i), covers the eighteenth century.)

Rupert E. Davis, <u>Methodism</u>, 1963 (and later) (a useful introduction to the origin and character of Methodism).

III STUDIES OF WESLEY AND OTHER MEMBERS OF HIS FAMILY

Luke Tyerman, <u>The Life and Times of the Revd. John Wesley AM</u>, 3 volumes, 1870 (and later editions). An old biography but full of interesting detail.

G. Elsie Harrison, <u>Son to Susanna</u> 1937, (Penguin ed. 1944).

H. Rack, <u>Reasonable Enthusiast, John Wesley and the Rise of Methodism</u> 1989 (revised 1992, 2002).

M. Piette, <u>John Wesley in the Evolution of Protestantism</u>, 1937.

(Detailed and comprehensive. The Bibliography is arranged chronologically and contains everything of importance written about Wesley up to the mid-1930s. All the earlier lives of Wesley are listed there.)

Stanley Ayling, <u>John Wesley</u>, 1979.

(A workmanlike biography).

V. H. H. Green, <u>The Young Mr. Wesley</u>, 1961.

(Excellent on Wesley's progress up to his conversion in 1738.)

John Pudney, <u>John Wesley and His World</u>, 1978

(Valuable for its illustrations).

Maldwyn Edwards, <u>John Wesley and the Eighteenth Century</u>, 1933.

John Vickers, <u>John Wesley, Founder of Methodism</u>, 1977.

(A Ladybird book. An admirable short, clear account. Illustrated.)

John A. Newton, _Susanna Wesley and the Puritan Tradition in Methodism_, 1968.
(On Wesley's mother).

Maldwyn Edwards, _My Dear Sister – The Story of John Wesley and the Women in his Life_, 1980.

Thomas Jackson, _The Life of the Reverend Charles Wesley, M.A._, 2 vols. 1841.
(A rich source of information on Charles, and on early Methodism in general.)

Frank Baker, _Charles Wesley as revealed by his Letters,_ 1948.
(An excellent account).

IV NORTH-EASTERN METHODISM

W. W. Stamp, _The Orphan House of Wesley with Notices of Early Methodism in Newcastle upon Tyne and its Vicinity_, 1863.
(A rich repository of information).

H. Pollard, _John Wesley in Northumberland_, 1949.
(Short but useful).

K. Tibbetts, 'Methodism in Berwick upon Tweed' in _Proceedings of the Wesley Historical Society_, xxxii, pt. 8, Dec. 1962.

T. J. Howells, _The Scarecrow Still Stands Mr Wesley: Alnwick Chapel 1786-1986_, 1986.

F. F. Bretherton, 'The Kingswood of the North' (early Methodism in Gateshead), _Proceedings of the Wesley Historical Society_, xx, pt. 6, June 1936.

F. F. Bretherton, 'John Wesley's Visits to Sunderland' and 'John Wesley's Visits to Monkwearmouth' in _Antiquities of Sunderland_, vol. xx, 1951, and vol. xxi, 1954.

J. G. Holmes, _Wesley and Wearmouth_, 1974.

Charles Wilson, _Wesleyan Methodism in the Chester-le-Street Circuit_, 1923.

F. Young, *The Early History of Methodism around Houghton le Spring*, 1927.

T. C. Dale, *The Durham Associations of John Wesley*, 1910.

William Thwaites, *Wesleyan Methodism in Durham City*, 1909.

W. R. Owen, *Methodism in the Hartlepools*, 1912.

G. Jackson, *Wesleyan Methodism in the Darlington Circuit*, 1850.

G. W. Wetherill, *The Story of Darlington Methodism*, 1950.

J. Wright, *Early Methodism in Yarm*, 1949.

H. L. Beadle, *Methodism in Richmond, 1750-1950*, 1984.

The above works deal with early Methodism mainly in an urban setting. Those following are concerned with Methodism in rural and upland areas:

T. J. Evans and T. A. Henderson, *Allendale Methodist Bicentenary, 1749-1947*, 1974.

J. Uren, *Methodism in Burnopfield, 1746-1906*, 1906.

T. W. Blanshard, *Sketch of Methodism in the Shotley Bridge Circuit*, 1872.

Anon, *High House Methodist Church, Weardale, 1760-1960*, 1960.

T. A. Milburn, *Life and Times in Weardale 1840-1910*, 1987.

Anthony Steele, *History of Methodism in Barnard Castle and the Principal Places in the Dales Circuit*, 1867 (A very valuable source.)

H. L. Beadle, *Newbiggin Chapel* (in Teesdale) 1981.

Margaret Batty, *Bygone Reeth: Reeth and Reeth Methodism*, 1985.

Margaret Batty, *Gunnerside Chapel and Gunnerside Folk*, 1967.

Margaret Batty, *A View of Arkengarthdale*, 1982.

John Ward, _Methodism in Swaledale and Neighbourhood_, 1865.

John Burgess, _John Wesley and Cumbria_, 1979.

John Burgess, _The Lake Counties and Christianity_, 1984.

V OTHER WORKS

George Dolbey, _The Architectural Expression of Methodism_, 1964. _(An interesting pioneer study in Methodist chapel styles)._

P. A. G. Clack and R. E. Pattinson, _Weardale Chapels,_ 1978. _(A gazetteer with illustrations and brief descriptions of all the chapels of Weardale)._

Wesley F. Swift, _How to Write a Local History of Methodism_, 1964. _(Revised editions 1972 and 1981)._

Tom Shaw, _John Wesley and Methodism – a Guide for Schools_, 1977.

(The two above works are very valuable publications of the (National) Wesley Historical Society.)

VI GENERAL HISTORIES of the North-East _(in which Methodism is mentioned, or which offer valuable information on the context of early Methodism)._

The following list is highly selective and is meant to indicate the kind of sources available.

T. Eden, _Durham_ 2 vols., county history, 1952.

W. Fordyce, _History and Antiquities of County Durham_, 2 vols., 1857.

E. Mackenzie, _A Descriptive and Historical Account of Newcastle_, 2 vols. in one, 1827.

E. Mackenzie, _A Historical, Topographical and Descriptive View of the County of Northumberland_, 2 vols., 1825.

W. Page (ed.) _Victoria County History; Durham_, especially vol. 2, 1907.

G. Tate, *History of Alnwick*, 2 vols., 1866-69.

J. Fuller, *History of Berwick on Tweed*, 1799.

S. Middlebrooke, *Newcastle upon Tyne*, 1950.

F. Manders, *History of Gateshead*, 1973.

G. B. Hodgson, *The Borough of South Shields*, 1903.

G. Garbutt, *History of Sunderland*, 1819.

M. Clay, G. E. Milburn and S. T. Miller, *Rain's Eye Plan of Sunderland*, 1984.

G. Dickinson, *Allendale and Whitfield*, 1903.

J. R. Featherston, *Weardale Men and Manners*, 1840.

T. A. Milburn, *Life and Times in Weardale 1840-1910*, 1987.

C.J. Hunt, *Lead Miners of the Northern Pennines*, 1970.

R. Fieldhouse and B. Jennings, *A History of Richmond and Swaledale*, 1978.

VII JOURNALS

Proceedings of the Wesley Historical Society – the journal of the national Wesley Historical Society published from 1897 to the present. Currently edited by E. Alan Rose. From time to time publishes items specifically relevant to the north-east. Indexes are published annually.

Bulletin of the North East Branch of the Wesley Historical Society, published twice yearly since 1962. Editorial Secretary, Andrea I. Milburn.

Journal of the Cumbrian Branch of the Wesley Historical Society, edited by Eddy Leteve.

JOHN WESLEY'S
NORTH-EASTERN ITINERARY

1742-90

with the details of visits made
to the Tyne and Wear area
by Charles Wesley 1742-51

It is the aim of this section to provide details of John Wesley's travels and the dates of his visits to particular places in the north-east of England (the old counties of Durham and Northumberland with some adjoining areas). Since the evangelistic initiative in these parts rested at first as much with Charles Wesley as with John, his visits (between 1742 and 1751) have been included within the itinerary, interspersed with those of John but separately numbered, and bracketed.

Despite the summarised form of presentation (and maybe even because of it) any reader, with the exercise of a little imagination, can glimpse in these pages something of the heroic scope of the work of the Wesleys, surely one of the most remarkable endeavours in Christian history. To help this, some brief explanatory notes and human touches have been added, particularly for the earlier visits. The principal sources of information have naturally been the journals of John and Charles Wesley, with the addition of the complete itinerary of John Wesley's travels published in 1908 in the Proceedings of the Wesley Historical Society. Certain corrections and clarifications, and at least one addition, have been made to the information gleaned form these sources, and it is hoped that the finished result represents an accurate and clear statement.

The map locates the places mentioned in the text but for a variety of reasons it is confined largely to County Durham and the Tyne valley, the areas to which, in fact, the bulk of the itinerary refers. Also shown are the sites of Methodist meeting houses existing in Wesley's lifetime or built immediately after he died (in 1791).

The vast majority of the places recorded here are those where the Wesleys actually preached rather than being simply staging posts on their journeys. It is obvious that certain places which they passed through were not recorded in their journals and either they did not stop there, or if they did, failed to note the fact. Where they stayed in a place for any length of time (a day or more) they would generally preach more than once; the frequency of these repeated preachings has not been noted in the itinerary. It is a general rule that when Wesley was travelling, the last place mentioned for each day was the one at which he spent the night.

Acknowledgements are gratefully extended to the Revd. Dr. J. C. Bowmer for supplying the details of Charles Wesley's north-eastern visits.

G. E. Milburn

I The early visits of John and Charles Wesley and the first Methodist Societies in the North-East 1742-47

1st Visit – 1742

(John Wesley's first visit to the 'colliers in the north' may have been suggested to him by the Countess of Huntingdon; certainly when he arrived in Newcastle he was accompanied by one of her preachers. But Newcastle's similarity to Bristol (where he had established an important Methodist centre), and the evangelistic opportunities offered by the north-east, were sufficient motivation. The warm response which he won in the north-east speedily convinced him of the rightness of his action and Newcastle became his strategic centre for the evangelisation of the northern counties. It is worth noting that Wesley's brother-in-law, Westley Hall, had visited Newcastle on a preaching tour in 1740, apparently without much consequence.)

27th May Wesley left Birstal, Yorkshire, to travel to Newcastle which he reached on the 28th. 28th-31st stayed in the town. Preached his first sermon on Sunday 30th May in Sandgate, a spot marked by the present obelisk. 31st left Newcastle for Boroughbridge.

(Charles Wesley's 1st visit – 1742

During the autumn of 1742 Charles Wesley spent some weeks in Newcastle, preaching to huge crowds in Sandgate and forming a Society which soon grew to 250. He preached in Newgate prison and the Keelmen's Hospital, and visited neighbouring places – Swalwell, Tanfield, Whickham and Ryton, at some of which Societies were also formed. He strongly urged John Wesley to follow up this work but left a few days before his brother arrived. There is no record of this visit in Charles' journal. See W. Stamp The Orphan House of Wesley, 1863 pp.4-10).

2nd Visit – 1742

13th November, John Wesley arrived in Newcastle from the south. Stayed until 30th December. Also visited, and preached at, Whickham 26th Nov., Tanfield Lea 28th Nov., Horsley 15th and 27th Dec., Swalwell 28th Dec., Tanfield Lea 29th Dec.

In Newcastle Wesley preached often at the Keelmen's Hospital and in the Society's first meeting room. Before he left Newcastle work had begun on the construction of the Orphan House (a combination of meeting house, school and preachers' quarters) on what is now Northumberland Street. 30th Dec. left Newcastle for Darlington. 31st to Boroughbridge.

3rd Visit – 1743

18th Feb. left Boroughbridge for Newcastle. 19th Feb. to 7th Apr. in Newcastle with preaching visits to Horsley 28th Feb., Pelton 1st and 17th March, Chowden (Gateshead Fell) 8th and 14th March, Tanfield 13th March, South Biddick 22nd March, Birtley 26th March, Plessey 1st and 3rd-4th April (Easter). In addition Wesley says he paid weekly visits to Chowden and probably Horsley, Pelton and Tanfield, all colliery communities. (The Newcastle Society was now some 800 strong and on 22nd February Wesley published in Newcastle the first edition of his Rules for the Societies).

(Charles Wesley's 2nd Visit – 1743

30th May arrived Newcastle, staying to 21st June and visiting Pelton 1st June, Chowden and Tanfield 5th and 12th June (Sundays), South Biddick 14th June, Plessey 15th June (through bitter weather), Sunderland, South Shields and North Shields 16th

June, Swalwell 19th June. (At North Shields Charles was 'met by a mob with a minister at their head'.) In Newcastle he preached in the Orphan House and 21st June left Newcastle).

4th Visit – 1743

29th June arrived Newcastle from Yorkshire, and stayed to 18th July paying preaching visits to Chowden 10th July, Sunderland 11th, Plessey 13th and 17th, Lower Spen 14th (where John Brown was now living and preaching). His open-air preaching at these places included sermons on the Sandhill, Newcastle and in Sunderland High Street. 18th July left Newcastle (with John Downes of Horsley) for Ferryhill, Darlington and Sandhutton.

5th Visit – 1743

31st Oct. arrived in Newcastle from Yorkshire (Wensleydale) and stayed until 21st Nov. Attended St. Nicholas' and St. Andrew's Churches on Sunday, 6th November. Visited Penshaw 13th Nov., Tanfield 14th, Horsley 15th, Plessey 16th, Spen 17th – preaching and ordering the Societies. 21st Nov. left Newcastle for Yorkshire.

(Charles Wesley's 3rd Visit – 1744

18th Feb. arrived Newcastle staying until 8th March and preaching also at Tanfield 26th Feb., Horsley 27th, Biddick 28th, Plessey 29th, Spen 1st March, Whickham 2nd March. 'A mob about our house' in Newcastle on 26th Feb. 8th March left Newcastle).

6th Visit – 1744

21st May arrived in Newcastle from Wensleydale, staying until 11th June. 21st-27th 'a quiet week'. 28th – 2nd June visited the classes in the town; 3rd-8th June visited those in the neighbouring country places. 10th June (a Sunday) preached at Biddick, Tanfield, Spen and Newcastle. 11th June left Newcastle for Durham where he met John Nelson and Thomas Beard (who had been impressed into the army), two of his lay preachers.

(Charles Wesley's 4th Visit – 1744

5th Nov. arrived Newcastle, staying to 13th Dec. Visited Tanfield 6th Nov., Burnopfield 15th Nov., Biddick 17th Nov., Sunderland 18th (walking there and back through violent hail and snow storms),

Whickham and Horsley 19th Nov., back to Newcastle 20th ('up to my middle in snow') and on to Plessey the same day. Whickham and Spen 22nd Nov., Biddick 27th Nov., and Burnopfield 9th Dec. (walking with a strained leg). 13th Dec. left Newcastle).

7th Visit – 1745

23rd Feb., arrived Newcastle from Sandhutton through terrible weather conditions ('the ground like glass'; Gateshead Fell 'a pathless waste of white'). 23rd Feb. to 15th April in Newcastle. Worked hard to reconcile some Society members who had fallen out, and visited the sick. During the week beginning 18th March visited 'the societies in the country'. On Easter Day the Newcastle Society worshipped at 4a.m. and Wesley preached at South Biddick at 7a.m. Father Adams, the Roman Catholic priest from Osmotherley, stayed with Wesley in Newcastle 28th March to 8th April. 15th April left Newcastle in the early morning, preached at Chester-le-Street at 8a.m. (in the street), took refreshment at Darlington and rode on to Northallerton where Fr. Adams persuaded him to turn aside to Osmotherley where he preached late that night and at 5a.m. on the 16th. (Elizabeth Tyerman baptised.)

8th Visit – 1745

16th-18th Sept. in Osmotherley; visited Mount Grace Priory and its Lady Chapel (with Fr. Adams?). 18th Sept. to Newcastle, staying until 4th Oct. Great anxiety in the city over the Jacobite Rising under Bonnie Prince Charlie; fears of an attack. Pilgrim Street gate walled up – the Orphan House was outside the walls. Wesley wrote to the Mayor (21st Sept.) professing his loyalty but also calling for a check to the 'flagrant wickedness' in the streets of the town. He preached in Gateshead 22nd and 29th Sept., and visited some of the country societies 30th Sept.-4th Oct. 9th Oct. left Newcastle; preached in Gateshead, and rode on to Sandhutton.

9th Visit – 1745

21st Oct. Osmotherley with Fr. Adams. 22nd Oct. to Newcastle – 'all things calm and quiet'. Wesley wrote to Alderman Ridley complaining of the morals of the troops in Newcastle and offered to preach to them (which he later did near their camp on the

Town Moor). Visited Biddick 28th Oct. 4th Nov. left Newcastle for Yorkshire.

10th Visit – 1746

26th Feb. arrived Newcastle from Keighley, staying to 17th March. Visited the sick. Preached at Whickham and Spen 5th March, Burnopfield 6th, Plessey 8th, Horsley 10th, Biddick 11th, Sunderland 12th. 17th March left Newcastle (with Mr. Downes and Mr. Shepherd) for Yorkshire.

(Charles Wesley's 5th Visit – 1746

23rd Oct. arrived Newcastle, staying to 30th Dec. Visited Whickham 31st Oct., Biddick 4th Nov., Plessey, Swalwell and Whickham 7th Nov., Burnopfield 9th Nov., Newlands 13th Nov., Biddick 17th Nov., Hexham 27th and 28th Nov., (at invitation of Dissenting minister – preached in a cock pit), Ryton 5th Dec., Whickham and Swalwell 14th Dec., Spen 16th Dec., Hexham 18th-19th Dec., Pelton 27th, Biddick 29th. 30th Dec. left Newcastle. At Ferryhill 'I preached and distributed books to a few starved souls').

11th Visit – 1747

1st-2nd March Osmotherley. 2nd March to Newcastle staying until 20th April. Met the stewards and examined the classes – the Society now reduced to 400. Preached at Gateshead 8th Mar. Examined the Societies round Newcastle; much travelling. Visited Blanchland 24th March (preached in the churchyard to a congregation mainly of lead miners), Newlands 24th (a Society formed by John Brown), South Biddick 29th, Sunderland 29th-31st, Winlaton Mill 1st April, Hexham and Horsley 5th, Rainton 6th, Dent's Hole (Byker) 7th, Blanchland and Spen 8th, Winlaton Mill 9th, Biddick and Picktree 11th, Gateshead and Swalwell 12th and 19th (the latter being Easter Day). 20th left Newcastle after preaching in the Orphan House to 'some of the finest people I had ever seen'; preached at Rainton at 9a.m. and reached Osmotherley by 6p.m. where John Nelson met him and recounted the persecution he had endured in York.

II Consolidation of the Societies in the Tyne-Wear-Derwent area. Extension into East and North Northumberland, Scotland and Cumbria 1748-51.

12th Visit – 1748

9th July arrived Newcastle from Boroughbridge. 13th-15th examined the Newcastle classes; and also spent time visiting the country Societies in the period 9th-16th July. 18th began a preaching tour into parts of Northumberland he had not visited before. 18th Morpeth and Widdrington. 19th Alnmouth and Alnwick. 20th-21st Berwick (when he preached to 2,000 people, 'serious and decent but not easily to be convinced of anything'). 22nd Tughall (near Bamburgh) and Alnwick. 23rd Longhorsley and Newcastle. 24th-26th in Newcastle. 27th Blanchland (preached to many lead miners) and Hindley Hill in Allendale – the farm which was an important Methodist base in Wesley's day. 28th Nenthead, Alston and Hindley Hill. 29th Allendale Town – a large congregation of miners as it was the bi-annual pay day. 30th Newlands and Tanfield Cross, and back to Newcastle, staying until 8th Aug. Visited Sunderland 31st, Biddick and Pelton 2nd Aug., Spen 4th and Horsley 5th. (Severe headache troubled Wesley 1st-6th Aug., when he cured it with ipecacuanha). 8th set out once more for the north – Morpeth and Alnwick. 9th Tughall and Berwick (to 11th). 11th Alnmouth and Widdrington. 12th back to Newcastle (reading Homer's Iliad). 16th left Newcastle (accompanied by Grace Murray); preached in Stockton market-place (a 'very large and very rude congregation') and Yarm (also in the market-place); reached Osmotherley by evening, where he also preached at 7p.m.

(Though not set out in detail, Wesley, of course, also preached regularly in Newcastle whenever he was there, either in the Orphan House or in the open air. A popular open-air site was the Castle Garth. This note applies to most of the entries relating to stays in Newcastle.)

13th Visit – 1749

5th Sept. Osmotherley. 6th to Newcastle (until 8th). 8th set out to visit the northern Societies. 8th Morpeth and Alnwick. 9th-14th Berwick, (a Society now founded). 14th Alnwick ('a stupid, drowsy people'). 15th Widdrington. 16th Morpeth, Plessey and

Newcastle. 16th-20th in Newcastle. 20th set out 'to visit the western societies' (Grace Murray with him). 20th-21st Hindley Hill – left 21st for Whitehaven where he preached and worked among colliers until 26th. 26th to Keswick and 27th back to Hindley Hill where he learned that (through Charles' agency) Grace was lost to him. 28th a day of fasting and prayer with John Brown and Christopher Hopper. 29th left for Whitehaven and on to Yorkshire.

14th Visit – 1749

10th Oct. arrived Newcastle from Yorkshire. 10th-16th in Newcastle. 16th left for Sandhutton.

15th Visit – 1751

19th April to Hindley Hill from Gamblesby. 20th to Newcastle, until 22nd. 22nd Morpeth and Alnwick. 23rd Berwick. 24th to Scotland. 26th to Berwick. 27th-28th Alnwick. 28th Alnmouth and Widdrington. 29th Plessey and Newcastle. 29th April – 6th May in Newcastle. Visited Sheephill (Burnopfield) and Sunderland 4th May, and Penshaw 5th. 6th left Newcastle for Durham and Stockton. 7th to Yorkshire.

(Charles Wesley's 6th Visit – 1751

13th-14th Aug. to Sunderland (society of about 100). 14th to Newcastle, until 24th. Visited Horsley 21st. 24th-26th Durham – 'communicated at the abbey'. 26th left for Thirsk).

III Consolidation. Extension of the South Durham-North Yorkshire Societies. Forays into the Dales 1752-64.

16th Visit – 1752

28th April to Stockton from Osmotherley and Stokesley 29th Durham. 30th Newcastle, until 11th May. Visited Sunderland 9th May. 11th Morpeth. 11th-12th Alnwick. 13th-14th Berwick. 15th Alnmouth and Widdrington. 16th Plessey. 17th Gateshead and Newcastle. 17th-25th in Newcastle. Visited Newlands and Sheephill (Burnopfield) 18th, Whickham 19th, Biddick 20th, Gateshead Fell 23rd. 25th left Newcastle for Chester-le-Street,

Durham and Barnard Castle (to 26th). 26th Weardale and Allendale. 27th to Penrith.

17th Visit – 1753

24th April to Berwick from Edinburgh. 25th-28th Alnwick. 28th to Newcastle until 7th May. Visited Sunderland 29th April and Gateshead Fell 3rd May (in the preaching house). First Quarterly Meeting of Societies in and around Newcastle 4th. 7th May left Newcastle for Durham and Stockton and on to Yorkshire.

18th Visit – 1755

13th May to Newcastle from Northallerton (with his wife, the former Mrs. Vazeille, whom he had married Feb. 1751). 13th-26th in Newcastle. Visited Gateshead Fell 18th, Nafferton (near Horsley) 21st, Sheepshill and Chester-le-Street 24th, Sunderland 24th-25th. 26th Morpeth and Alnwick. 27th Newcastle – to 2nd June. 2nd to Durham (where Jacob Rowell had been preaching) and Osmotherley.

19th Visit – 1757

8th June to Berwick from Dunbar. 8th-9th Berwick. 10th Kelso. 11th Wooler and Alnwick. 11th-12th Alnwick. 13th Morpeth, Plessey and Newcastle. 13th-15th Newcastle. 16th-19th Sunderland. 19th South Shields and back to Newcastle, to 4th July. Visited Chester-le-Street 22nd, South Biddick and Sunderland 23rd, Swalwell 25th, Gateshead and Sheepshill 26th, Horsley and Prudhoe 27th, Gateshead 3rd July. 4th July to Durham and Hartlepool. 5th Stockton. 6th Yarm and Osmotherley. 7th Hawnby.

20th Visit – 1759

1st June Berwick (from Dunbar). 2nd-3rd Alnwick. 4th Plessey and Newcastle. 4th-16th in Newcastle. Visited Gateshead Fell 6th, Sunderland 9th, Gateshead, Chester-le-Street, Newlands and Sheephill 13th. 16th Widdrington and Alnwick, to 18th. 18th Morpeth, Plessey and back to Newcastle. 18th June-2nd July in and around Newcastle. Visited Gateshead 19th June, Nafferton 21st, Saltwick 22nd, Sunderland 23rd-24th, South and North Shields 24th, Swalwell 29th, Winlaton Mill and Sheephill 30th, Gateshead and the Fell 1st July. 2nd July left Newcastle for Durham and

Hartlepool. 2nd-4th Hartlepool. 4th-6th Stockton. 6th-7th Yarm. 7th to Hutton Rudby and Potto. 8th Stokesley, Guisborough and Robin Hood's Bay.

21st Visit – 1761

14th May Berwick (from Dunbar) and Alnwick. 14th-18th Alnwick, visiting Warkworth 16th and Alnmouth 17th. 18th Widdrington, Morpeth, Plessey, Newcastle. 18th-25th in and around Newcastle, visiting Gateshead Fell 19th, Plessey 23rd. 25th North Shields and South Shields (to 26th). 26th-31st Sunderland, visiting Monkwearmouth 27th and 31st, Biddick 28th. 31st back to Newcastle. 1st-4th June visited 'many little places round Newcastle' (and probably Durham). 5th Prudhoe and Nafferton. 6th Winlaton and Swalwell. 8th Hexham, Allendale and Weardale. 9th Teesdale and Swaledale. 10th Barnard Castle and Brancepeth. 12th Newcastle. 13th Sunderland. 14th Monkwearmouth, Gateshead Fell and Newcastle. 15th Durham and Hartlepool (to 17th), visiting Sheraton. 17th-19th Stockton. 19th The Grange, Darlington, and Yarm. 20th-22nd Hutton Rudby visiting Osmotherley and Potto. 22nd Stokesley and Guisborough. 23rd Whitby.

22nd Visit – 1763

18th May arrived Newcastle (from London) by post chaise. Travelled on north 'at leisure'. 21st arrived Edinburgh.

23rd Visit – 1763

31st May Alnwick, from Dunbar. 1st June Morpeth, Plessey, Newcastle. 1st-4th Newcastle. 4th-5th Sunderland, Monkwearmouth. 5th Newcastle. 6th-7th Barnard Castle. 7th-8th Yarm. 8th Potto, Thirsk, York.

24th Visit – 1764

20th-23rd April Whitby. 23rd Guisborough, Stokesley, Hutton Rudby. 24th Potto, and Yarm (in the new octagon Chapel). 26th-27th in Yarm; visited Stockton 24th. 27th Darlington and Barnard Castle. 28th April-8th May Newcastle. 8th Wolsingham and Barnard Castle. 9th Teesdale and Weardale. 10th Prudhoe, Nafferton and Newcastle. 10th-21st in the around Newcastle, visiting South and North Shields 15th, Plessey 19th, Gateshead and the Fell 20th. 21st Morpeth and Alnwick (to 22nd). 23rd Holy Island and Berwick. 24th Dunbar.

25th Visit – 1764

18th June Wooler, from Edinburgh, and Whittingham (by chaise). 19th Morpeth and Newcastle. 19th-21st Newcastle, visiting the Fell. 21st Carlisle. 22nd Whitehaven.

IV Consolidation of the Societies 1765-90

26th Visit – 1765

11th-13th April Kendal. 13th-15th Barnard Castle. 15th-22nd Newcastle visiting Durham and the Fell 18th. 22nd Alnwick and Berwick (by chaise). 23rd Dunbar and Edinburgh.

27th Visit – 1765

7th-8th Aug. to Newcastle (overnight) from Carlisle. 8th-13th in and around Newcastle visiting Gateshead Fell and Hartley 11th, Sunderland 12th. 13th Durham and Yarm. 14th Leeds.

28th Visit – 1766

29th April Thirsk and Yarm. 30th-6th May Newcastle, visiting Gateshead Fell 4th May. 6th-12th Sunderland and Monkwearmouth (preaching several times at St. Peter's). 12th South and North Shields, and back to Newcastle. 12th-19th in Newcastle, preaching 'at neighbouring places'. 19th Plessey and Morpeth. 20th Felton and Alnwick, to 22nd. 22nd Belford and Berwick. 23rd to Scotland.

29th Visit –1766

25th-30th June Whitehaven. 30th Penrith, Appleby and Brough. 1st-2nd July Barnard Castle. 2nd Teesdale and Upper Weardale. 3rd Wolsingham and Newcastle, to 5th. 5th-6th Sunderland. 6th Gateshead and Newcastle. 7th Durham and Hartlepool. 8th Stockton. 9th Yarm. 10th Potto, Hutton Rudby.

30th Visit – 1767

6th Aug. Newcastle, from Dunbar. 6th-10th Newcastle, visiting Monkwearmouth and Gateshead Fell 9th. 11th ? in Durham. 12th Grantham (on way to London by coach).

31st Visit – 1768

18th May Berwick, from Dunbar. 19th-21st Alnwick. 21st Morpeth and Newcastle. 21st-24th in Newcastle, visiting Gateshead and the Fell 22nd. 25th-31st Sunderland (took down Elizabeth Hobson's account of paranormal experiences). 31st Weardale ('a little excursion'). 1st June Teesdale and Barnard Castle. 2nd Brough and Swaledale (?Low Row). 3rd Richmond, Barnard Castle, Newcastle. 3rd-13th in and around Newcastle, visiting Plessey and Hartley 5th, South Shields (by water) and Tynemouth 7th. 13th left Newcastle. 14th Norton (near Stockton). 17th Osmotherley (probably in Yarm and Hutton Rudby en route).

32nd Visit – 1770

19th May Berwick (from Dunbar) and Alnwick. 19th-21st Alnwick. 21st Morpeth and Newcastle to 22nd. 23rd-27th Sunderland, visiting North Biddick (by boat) 26th. 27th Gateshead and Newcastle, to 28th. 29th May-1st June Weardale, Teesdale and Swaledale ('a little circuit'). 2nd-11th June in and around Newcastle, visiting Sunderland 3rd-4th. (This visit to Sunderland not recorded in the Journal. See F. F. Bretherton in Antiquities of Sunderland Vol. XX p.135.) 11th Durham and Stockton (new preaching house). 12th Stockton, Norton, Yarm. 13th Hartley, Thirsk. 14th Potto, Hutton Rudby. 15th Whitby.

33rd Visit – 1772

23rd Alnwick (from Scotland) to 25th. 25th Morpeth and Newcastle. 25th-27th Newcastle. 27th-31st Sunderland. 31st Gateshead Fell, Newcastle. 1st-4th June 'a little tour through the dales' – 1st Kiphill, Wolsingham, Barnard Castle. 2nd Newbiggin (Teesdale) and High House (Weardale). 2nd-5th Weardale (account of the Weardale revival). 5th Newcastle. 5th-15th in and around Newcastle visiting 'many places' including Sunderland 13th. 15th Durham and Stockton. 16th Yarm. 17th Thirsk. 18th Osmotherley and Hutton Rudby. 19th Stokesley, Castleton, Whitby.

34th Visit – 1774

9th June Alnwick, from Dunbar. 10th Morpeth and Newcastle. 11th-12th Weardale (Wolsingham and High House). 13th Teesdale and Swaledale (?Low Row). 14th Wensleydale (Redmire), Richmond, Barnard Castle. 15th Durham and Sunderland. 15th-19th Sunderland, visiting Biddick 18th. 19th Gateshead Fell and Newcastle. 19th-27th Newcastle, visiting Horsley 20th. 27th Durham and Stockton. 28th Yarm (Wesley's 71st birthday). 29th Osmotherley and Thirsk. 30th Hutton Rudby. 1st July, Stokesley, Guisborough, Whitby.

35th Visit – 1776

30th May Alnwick, from Dunbar. 31st Morpeth. 1st June Newcastle. 1st-5th Newcastle, visiting Sunderland 3rd. 6th Darlington and Barnard Castle. 7th Teesdale and Weardale. 8th Sheepshill (Burnopfield) and Newcastle. 8th-17th Newcastle. 17th Durham and Darlington to 18th. 19th Osmotherley. 24th Scarborough.

36th Visit – 1777

28th April left London by coach for north. 30th-4th May Newcastle, visiting Sunderland 3rd. 5th Durham and Darlington to 7th. 7th Yarm. 8th Osmotherley (death of Fr. Adams).

37th Visit – 1779

7th May Darlington, from Yorkshire. 7th-10th Darlington. 10th-11th Barnard Castle. 11th Brough. 12th Cotherstone, Newbiggin (looked at High Force), Weardale. 13th-17th in and round Newcastle, visiting Gateshead Fell and Sheephill (a new preaching house) 16th. 17th North Shields and Sunderland. 17th-20th Sunderland and Monkwearmouth. 20th-24th Newcastle, visiting Gateshead Fell 23rd. 24th Plessey, Morpeth, Alnwick. 25th Berwick. 26th Dunbar, 27th Edinburgh.

38th Visit – 1779

21st June Alnwick, from Dunbar. 22nd-24th Newcastle. 24th Stockton and Yarm. 25th Potto, Hutton Rudby. 26th Stokesley, Guisborough, Whitby.

39th Visit – 1780

2nd May Ripon (visiting Jervaulx Abbey). 3rd Swaledale (by horse, the chaise sent round) and Barnard Castle. 4th Cotherstone, Newbiggin, Weardale, 5th Nenthead, Gamblesby, Penrith. 5th-10th Whitehaven, Cockermouth, etc. 11th Newcastle (from Carlisle) to 12th. 12th-14th Sunderland. 14th Gateshead, Newcastle. 15th left Newcastle for the north. 16th Berwick. 17th Dunbar.

40th Visit – 1781

16th June Newcastle, from Carlisle. 16th-20th Newcastle, visiting Gateshead 17th. 20th-22nd Sunderland and Monkwearmouth. 22nd Newcastle. 23rd Hexham. 24th Greenside (many Catholics heard Wesley preach), Gateshead Fell, Newcastle. 25th-27th travelled to Thirsk and York, 'preaching at many places on the way'.

41st Visit - 1782

25th May Sunderland, from the south. 26th Newcastle. 27th set out for Scotland. 28th Alnwick, 29th Dunbar.

42nd Visit – 1784

26th May Berwick, from Dunbar. 27th Kelso. 28th Alnwick. 29th Morpeth and Newcastle. 29th-3rd June in and round Newcastle, visiting Gateshead Fell 30th, Howden Pans and North Shields, 1st June. 4th Sunderland (by chaise) to 6th (portrait painted by Thomas Horsley). 7th Durham (chaise) and Hartlepool. 8th Stockton and Yarm. 9th Darlington, Barnard Castle. 10th Cotherstone, Newbiggin, Weardale. 11th Newbiggin, Middleton in Teesdale, Barnard Castle (the dales tour was on horseback). 12th-14th Northallerton, Thirsk. 15th Osmotherley, Potto, Hutton Rudby. 16th Stokesley, Guisborough, Whitby.

43rd Visit – 1786

8th May Easingwold, Thirsk. 9th Richmond. 10th Barnard Castle. 11th Brough, Appleby, Penrith. 12th Carlisle. 13th to Scotland (Glasgow, etc.).

44th Visit – 1786

31st May Berwick, from Dunbar. 1st-2nd June Alnwick (foundation stone of preaching house). 2nd Morpeth and Newcastle. 2nd-7th Newcastle, visited Gateshead Fell 4th. 7th North Shields, South Shields, Sunderland. 7th-8th Sunderland and Monkwearmouth. 9th Durham, Hartlepool. 10th-11th Darlington. 12th Stockton, Yarm. 13th Hutton Rudby, Guisborough, Whitby.

45th Visit – 1788

23rd May Berwick, from Dunbar. 24th-26th Alnwick. 26th Morpeth, Newcastle. 26th-29th ? in Newcastle. 30th-31st North Shields. 31st South Shields and Sunderland. 1st-3rd June Sunderland and Monkwearmouth. 3rd-5th Newcastle. 5th Kip Hill, Wolsingham, upper Weardale, (by chaise – the first in Weardale?). 6th-7th Stanhope. 7th Burnopfield, Newcastle. 7th-9th Newcastle and Gateshead. 9th Durham, West Auckland, Barnard Castle. 10th Darlington. 11th Stockton, Yarm. 12th Potto, Hutton Rudby. 13th Stokesley, Guisborough, Whitby.

46th Visit – 1790

2nd June Carlisle, from Dumfries. 3rd Brampton, Haltwhistle, Hexham (new house). 4th-9th Newcastle, visiting Gateshead Fell 6th. 10th Wolsingham and upper Weardale. 11th Stanhope, Wolsingham, Durham. 12th-14th Sunderland, Monkwearmouth, the Panns. 14th Castle Eden, Hartlepool. 15th Stockton, Norton, Yarm (to 16th). 17th Potto, Hutton Rudby. 18th Stokesley, Whitby.

(Wesley died in London on 2nd March, 1791, aged 87 years).

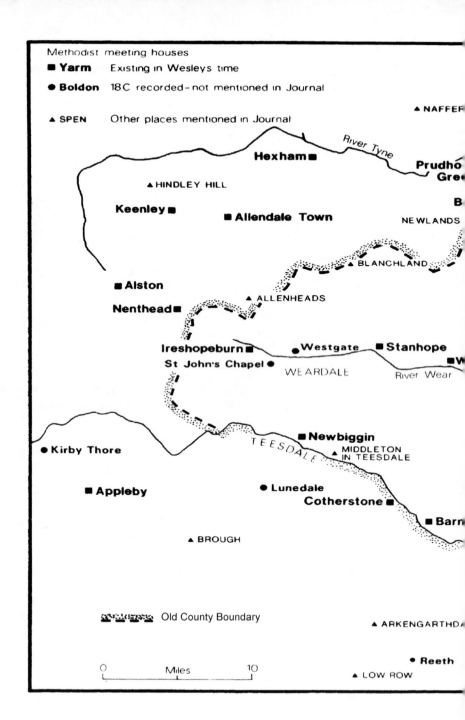

Methodist meeting houses

■ **Yarm**   Existing in Wesleys time

● **Boldon**   18C recorded – not mentioned in Journal

▲ SPEN   Other places mentioned in Journal

▲ NAFFER

River Tyne

Hexham■

Prudhó
Gre

▲ HINDLEY HILL

B

Keenley■

■ **Allendale Town**

NEWLANDS

▲ BLANCHLAND

■ **Alston**

▲ ALLENHEADS

Nenthead■

Ireshopeburn■   ●**Westgate** ■**Stanhope**

St John's Chapel ●   WEARDALE   ■**W**

River Wear

■**Newbiggin**

TEESDALE   ▲ MIDDLETON
IN TEESDALE

●**Kirby Thore**

■ **Appleby**   ●**Lunedale**
Cotherstone■

■**Barn**

▲ BROUGH

▓▓▓▓▓ Old County Boundary

▲ ARKENGARTHD

0   Miles   10

● **Reeth**

▲ LOW ROW

120

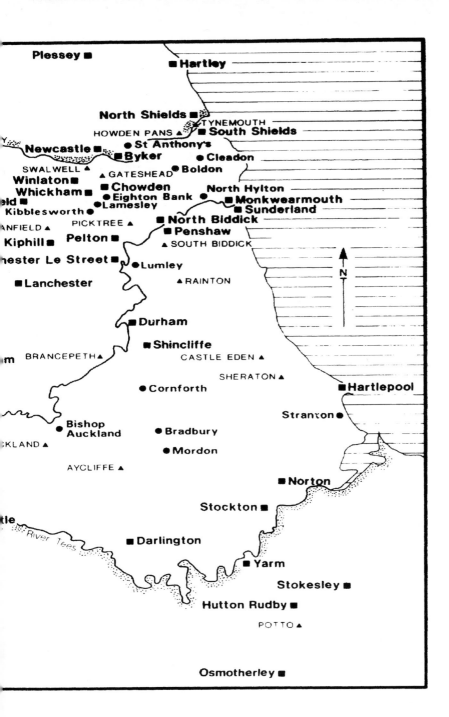

Plessey ■
■ Hartley

North Shields ■
TYNEMOUTH
HOWDEN PANS ▲ ■ South Shields
Y. Newcastle ■ ● St Anthony's
SWALWELL ▲ ■ Byker ● Cleadon
Winlaton ■ ▲ GATESHEAD ● Boldon
Whickham ■ ● Chowden
eld ■ ● Eighton Bank North Hylton ●
Kibblesworth ● ■ Lamesley ■ Monkwearmouth
ANFIELD ▲ PICKTREE ▲ ■ North Biddick ■ Sunderland
Kiphill ■ Pelton ■ ■ Penshaw
hester Le Street ■ ▲ SOUTH BIDDICK
■ Lanchester ● Lumley
▲ RAINTON

■ Durham
■ Shincliffe
m BRANCEPETH ▲ CASTLE EDEN ▲
SHERATON ▲
● Cornforth ■ Hartlepool
Stranton ●
Bishop ● Bradbury
Auckland
:KLAND ▲ ● Mordon
AYCLIFFE ▲
■ Norton
Stockton ■
tle
River Tees ■ Darlington
■ Yarm
Stokesley ■
Hutton Rudby ■
POTTO ▲
Osmotherley ■

N